WILLIAM MORRIS IN APPLIQUÉ

MICHELE HILL

PHOTOGRAPHY BY ANDREW DUNBAR

First published in 2009 by C&T Publishing,
PO Box 1456, Lafayette, CA 94549
Text and Artwork ©2009 Country Bumpkin Publications

Publisher Amy Marson, C&T Publishing, Inc.

Author Michele Hill

Editor Anna Scott

Editorial Assistants Marian Carpenter, Heidi Reid, Joy Peters

Graphic design Lynton Grandison, Jenny James

Illustrations Jenny James

Pattern design Jennie Victorsen

Photography & Styling Andrew Dunbar Photography

10 9 8 7 6 5 4 3 2 1
ISBN-13: 978-1-57120-794-4
ISBN-10: 1-57120-794-5
Printed in China

We take great care to ensure that the information included in our
products is accurate and presented in good faith, but no warranty
is provided nor results guaranteed. Having no control over the
choices of materials or procedures used, neither the author nor
C&T Publishing, Inc., shall have any liability to any person or
entity with respect to any loss or damage caused directly or
indirectly by the information contained in this book. For your
convenience, we post an up-to-date listing of corrections on our
website (www.ctpub.com). If a correction is not already noted,
please contact our customer service department at
ctinfo@ctpub.com or at P.O. Box 1456, Lafayette, CA, 94549.

For a list of other fine books from C&T Publishing,
ask for a free catalog:
C&T Publishing, Inc.
P.O. Box 1456, Lafayette, CA 94549
Phone: (800) 284-1114 Email: ctinfo@ctpub.com
Website: www.ctpub.com

For quilting supplies:
Cotton Patch Mail Order
3405 Hall Lane, Dept. CTB, Lafayette, CA 94549
Phone: (800) 835-4418 or (925) 283-7883
Email: quiltusa@yahoo.com
Website: www.quiltusa.com

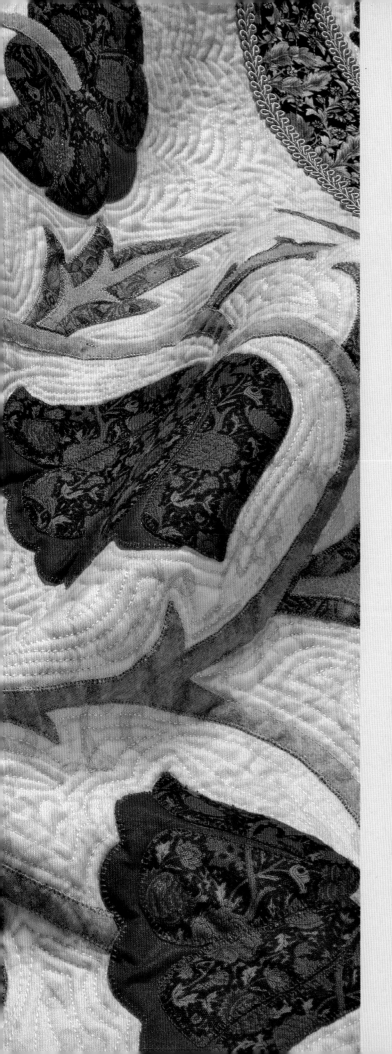

I dedicate this book to my wonderful

husband Larry and to our beautiful daughters

Emily and Sophie.

Thank you for putting up with my obsession

and especially Larry for being my best friend

and colour adviser.

Contents

Introduction

"Everything made by man's hand has a form which must be either beautiful or ugly; beautiful if it is in accord with nature and helps her; ugly if it is discordant with nature, and thwarts her. It cannot be indifferent." William Morris

William Morris was a weaver, illuminator, typographer, and designer of stained glass, tiles, furniture, tapestries and carpets. He formed the Society for the Protection of Ancient Buildings and was an environmentalist. He explored medieval craftsmanship and revived techniques of dying, printing and weaving.

Morris challenged mass produced mediocrity of the 19th century. With a commitment to socialist views he set out to improve working conditions for all. He rejected industrialisation and believed that work should be enjoyable and creative. His vision was for a future Britain where harmony with nature, art, morality and peace would rule. He was also instrumental in re-establishing the value of handcrafted work through improving the status and self-respect of the textile designer, printer and weaver. He inspired an entire generation of designers and architects in the field of the applied arts, insisting on integrating life with art, and art with life.

Over 100 years later William Morris continues to influence craftspeople and fabric designers. I first admired the designs of Morris when I visited the Victoria & Albert Museum in London in 1997. I sensed a familiarity with his interpretation of flowers and leaves and over time have come to admire his philosophy and ideals on life.

William Morris, portrait 1875

On my return home to Adelaide that same year, I discovered that we have a strong connection to Morris and that our very own Art Gallery of South Australia has one of the biggest collections of original Morris works outside of Britain.

MICHELE

William Morris

"If you want a golden rule that will fit everything, this is it: Have nothing in your houses that you do not know to be useful or believe to be beautiful." William Morris 1834 - 1896

William Morris was born in Essex on 24th March 1834. He was the third of nine children to parents William and Emma. Morris' father was a partner in a successful and prosperous firm of city financiers and brokers. A comfortable salary allowed the family the opportunity of moving to a grander home, Woodford Hall in 1840 when Morris was six years old. This Georgian residence was on the edge of Epping Forest where Morris spent many hours playing.

Morris' first biographer recorded that he was a precocious child who was reading Sir Walter Scott's novels at the age of four. He was given his own garden, which was sure to be the catalyst for a lifelong interest in botany and horticulture.

Morris' early schooling was at Preparatory School Walthamstow. He then moved on to Marlborough College, one of the new public schools that proliferated in the mid nineteenth century. Morris wrote in a letter in 1883 that Marlborough was:

"a very rough school. As far as my school instruction went, I think I may fairly say I learned next to nothing there, for indeed next to nothing was taught; but the place is in very beautiful country, thickly scattered over with prehistoric monuments, and I set myself eagerly to studying there and everything else that had any history in it, and so perhaps learnt a good deal."

Morris entered Oxford University in 1853 and it was here that he met Edward Burne-Jones (1833 - 1898), who was to become a life-long friend and business partner.

Morris and Burne-Jones expected Oxford to fulfill their religious career plans but found only apathy and indifference. They abandoned their plans to enter the church in 1855 and turned to examining medieval illuminated manuscripts. Together they became increasingly interested

in art and developed an admiration for the Middle Ages. Morris left university with a pass degree and became an apprentice to the Gothic revival architect, George Edmund Street (1824 - 1881). He began work in January 1856, staying only nine months. During this time he was to copy a detailed drawing of the doorway of Saint Augustine's, Canterbury. He found this tedious but it evidently influenced Morris with the view of architecture as the most important of the visual arts. Street's chief assistant was Philip Webb (1831 - 1915), who was to become Morris' own architect and co-worker in the Society for the Protection of Ancient Buildings.

Morris' artistic pursuits began with modelling in clay, carving in wood and stone and illuminating books. Morris was also part of a group of young artists that included Burne-Jones and painter Dante Gabriel Rossetti (1828 - 1882), who painted a series of murals on Arthurian subjects in the Oxford Union Societies Debating Hall, now the Oxford Library.

The Oxford mural was an amateur undertaking, embraced with much enthusiasm and commitment without any payment. The designing of the murals required models and Rossetti noticed a 17year-old girl Jane Burden, who typified the Pre-Raphaelite ideals of female beauty, with dark wavy hair, soulful eyes and attenuated pallor. She was pursued to model, and it was her beauty that captured Morris' admiration.

Morris & Company, London
Britain, 1861 - 1940
attributed to May Morris, designer
Britain, 1862 - 1938
Helen Elizabeth Dutton, embroiderer
Australia, c.1844 - 1901
Wild peony firescreen
c.1895, London and Kapunda
silk embroidery, walnut frame, glass
96.7 x 53.6 x 25.5cm
South Australian Government Grant 1978
Art Gallery of South Australia, Adelaide

Morris & Company, London, Britain, 1861 - 1940
J. H. Dearle, designer, Britain, 1860 - 1932
Jeffrey & Company, printer, Britain, 1836 - 1930
Celandine wallpaper c.1900, London, colour woodcut on paper
116 x 58.5cm, Ellen Christensen Bequest Fund 2002
Art Gallery of South Australia, Adelaide

The daughter of a stable hand, she became the love of Morris' life. They married in 1859 and had two daughters, Jane Alice 'Jenny' and Mary 'May'. May was the only daughter to marry, the marriage only lasting four years. A talented embroiderer and designer herself, she took a keen interest in her father's business and became the director of the embroidery department at the age of 23. She continued this right up to the 1930's.

Morris found it difficult to find suitable ready-made furniture when decorating his home, Red House. As a result he set about bringing together people skilled in the decorative arts, including his friends Burne-Jones, Rossetti and Phillip Webb and in January 1861 opened the business that was to become Morris & Co. Jointly they began to produce and sell painted furniture, stained glass and decorative tiles.

Morris & Co. often referred to as 'The Firm' had its first public display at the International Exhibition at South Kensington in 1862. Morris' stained glass was particularly well received, resulting in a number of commissions. As The Firm's reputation grew, interior decorating commissions became a substantial part of its services, often involving entire interior design make-overs. One major commission in 1880 was to decorate St James Palace, London. The silk *St James* was used in the council chamber room and throne room as was wallpaper of the same name. Morris & Co. became Morris' life and while writing and publishing poetry as well as becoming increasingly involved in politics, he created more than 600 designs including wallpapers, embroideries, woven and printed fabrics, tapestries, tiles, stained glass and carpets.

Maintaining the Pugin and Ruskin 'truth to nature' ethos and by using nature as his chief source of design, Morris' patterns are exquisite compositions of figurative and ornate leaves and flowers. His ability to create repeating patterns was one of his greatest talents. Morris took a keen interest in learning all techniques necessary for design and production in any medium, to the extent that he taught himself to weave, embroider and print.

In 1881 the workshops were moved from Queen Square to Merton Abbey, creating more space and eventually leading to an expansion of the business employing over one hundred workers within three years. Being an out-spoken socialist, Morris took a stand against oppressive factory conditions and was passionate that workers should have joy in their work. Merton Abbey was set up to function like the workshop of a skilled craftsman rather than a modern factory. Morris & Co. carried out production at Merton Abbey for over 60 years, until May 1940, just after the outbreak of World War II.

Morris had suffered gout since his early twenties. This, along with an infected kidney became seriously debilitating and Morris was told by his doctors that *"Henceforth he must consider himself an invalid to the extent of husbanding his strength and living under a very careful régime"*.

Life slowed down for Morris, and he was able to spend more time at Kelmscott Press producing illuminated manuscripts and books. In 1895 Morris wrote *"It was the essence of my undertaking to produce books which it would be a pleasure to look upon as pieces of printing and arrangement of type"*. These were happy years, free of the administration of The Firm and the busy schedule of his socialist crusade. He could spend his time doing the things he enjoyed, writing romances, designing fabrics and making beautiful books.

By the end of 1895 Morris was looking frail, losing weight and his untidy mop of hair was completely white. A leading physician diagnosed diabetes. On the 2nd of June the following year, Morris was to receive one of the first two copies of Chaucer and in July he indulged himself by purchasing an illuminated manuscript for £1000 – the largest sum he had ever spent. In August he took a cruise to Norway against his doctor's wishes, but returned early, writing to Webb, *"P.S. somewhat better, but hated the voyage; so glad to be home"*.

Morris was now too weak to write but completed 'The Sundering Flood' on the 8th of September by dictating. The following morning he signed his will and three days later a friend wrote in his diary *"Morris is dying, slowly. It is an astonishing spectacle. He sits speechless, waiting for the end to come"*. On Friday, 2nd October Morris could not recognize his oldest friend Burne-Jones. He died in the bedroom of his London home the following morning, aged 62 years.

Morris' simple funeral was held at Kelmscott in a little 12th century village church decorated for the Harvest Festival with pumpkins, apples and autumn leaves. Far removed from the grandeur of a funeral at St Paul's Cathedral or Westminster Abbey, his body was placed in an unpolished oak coffin and transported from his home to Paddington Station in a glass-sided hearse drawn by two horses. The train was met at Lechlade by a gaily-painted harvest-cart, decorated with vine leaves.

Edward Burne-Jones wrote that *"The burial was as sweet and touching as those others were foolish"*.

"The little wagon with its floor of moss and willow branches broke one's heart it was so beautiful – and of course there were no kings there – the king was being buried and there were no others left".

In the rain, his body was laid to rest in a corner of the churchyard beneath a starkly beautiful gravestone, designed by his faithful friend Philip Webb.

Morris & Company, London
Britain, 1861 - 1940
William Morris, designer
Britain, 1834 - 1896
Daisy tile panel c.1870s, London
earthenware tiles, hand painted
98.5 x 30.2 x 3.5cm
Mrs Mary Overton Gift Fund 2002
Art Gallery of South Australia, Adelaide

"Simply being William Morris, and having done more work than most ten men".

Quote from Morris' physician at the time of his death.

The Adelaide Connection

Many British clients commissioned Morris & Co. to produce major interior make-overs that included carpets, curtains, soft furnishings, wallpaper and furniture. However, many international clients also sought its services. During the 1880s and 1890s one of The Firm's most important clients was the Scottish born couple Robert Barr Smith (1824 - 1915) and his wife Joanna (1835 - 1919). Robert was reputed to be 'the richest man in Australasia' along with his business partner and brother-in-law Thomas Elder (1817 - 1897). They were involved in shipping, merchant, pastoral and mining interests in South Australia. This allowed Robert Barr Smith the privilege of purchasing extravagant homes, which were

decorated extensively with works by Morris & Co. One of these homes, their summer residence Auchendarroch at Mount Barker in the Adelaide Hills (now cinema and function centre) still has the original *Spring Thicket* wallpaper, faithfully restored, in the ballroom.

It is known that the Barr Smiths often travelled to Britain sometimes staying up to twelve months at a time. Research has not revealed the true connection between Morris and the Barr Smiths, although a letter that Robert wrote in 1881 to his London architect, records him asking him to look for soft furnishings including a Persian rug for the homes they were renovating in Adelaide. Morris & Co. had a solid base and reputation by this time and it may have been that the London

Large drawing-room, Torrens Park, Adelaide, c.1890.

architect had previously partnered with the company. It is also thought that one of Morris' daughters, May attended school with Mabel Barr Smith, one of Robert and Joanna's daughters.

For a period of forty-five years (1884 - 1929), three generations of Barr Smiths decorated at least seven houses in and around Adelaide. They not only purchased furniture, carpets, wallpapers and soft furnishings, they also purchased numerous embroidery works. The Barr Smith women were keen embroiderers and it is highly likely that May Morris, who was now in charge of the embroidery section of Morris & Co. became quite closely acquainted with both Joanna and Mabel Barr Smith through many purchases and correspondence. Some of these embroideries included screens, portieres, mantle borders, cushions, table covers and workbags. Embroideries were designed and named especially for the Australian clients, including a tablecover named *Australia*, designed by May Morris for Joanna to commemorate the centenary in 1888 and the *Adelaide* embroideries used for cushions and screen panels. It is said that the Barr Smiths were one of Morris & Co.'s best customers and because of this unique connection, Adelaide can now claim to own one of the biggest collections of Morris work outside of Britain.

Thirty-six furnishing fabrics and twenty wallpaper designs have been identified in Adelaide, South Australia, to date along with carpets, furniture and stained glass windows.

Ernest Gall, photographer
Robert and Joanna Barr Smith seated in the bay window of the drawing-room at Auchendarroch, Mount Barker, Adelaide Hills c.1897

Erlistoun Mitchell and screen embroidered by her with
Morris & Company's 'Adelaide' design
c.1906, Fitzroy, Adelaide
gelatin-silver photograph 10 x 12.5cm (sheet)
Gift of Joanna Simpson in memory of her mother Mrs J.R. Thomson 1990
Art Gallery of South Australia, Adelaide

My journey

I first started designing my own appliquéd quilts in 1992 often sourcing inspiration from antique quilts. To see the Morris textiles at the Victoria & Albert Museum in London some years ago was a life changing experience for me and has now become a major influence in my designing. On my return home to Adelaide, I discovered that the Art Gallery of South Australia has its own unique collection which is one of the biggest in the world outside of Britain. In 2002 the Gallery had an extended exhibition of the entire collection for all to view. As the collection is extensive, this was a rare occasion as usually only a very small part of it is ever on display at one time. It has since been exhibited in several states of Australia and recently in New Zealand.

Each of my quilt patterns has a strong connection to one or more of Morris' original designs. When I study his work and put pencil to paper, my wish is not to plagiarise his talent but simply to acknowledge his genius.

Morris & Company, London, Britain, 1861 - 1940
attributed to May Morris, designer, Britain, 1862 - 1938
Erlistoun Mitchell, embroiderer, Australia, 1868 - 1913
Adelaide [two panels from a screen]
c.1890, embroidered Adelaide
silk embroidery on silk 45.5 x 45.5cm (each)
Private Collection

Strawberry Thief (1998) is one of Morris' most well known designs and was the first Morris inspired quilt that I made. The original design created in 1883 reflects Morris' love of nature and birds and was the first indigo-discharge dyed and block printed chintz that Morris & Co. produced.

As this was my first attempt at making a Morris style quilt, I can now see that I lacked careful scrutiny of the finer details. The birds, in fact, have leaves in their beaks instead of strawberries. I am not sure why I did that now – my garden daisy leaves must have seemed an easier option! The thrushes, blue fern and flower features bear some resemblance to the original textile.

Top; **Strawberry Thief,** 1883. Printed chintz designed by William Morris. This was the first chintz to combine indigo-discharge-dyeing and block-printing with red and yellow at Merton Abbey.
Above; **Strawberry Thief,** printed cotton reproduction for patchwork and quilting.

Morris & Company, London
Britain, 1861 - 1940
J. H. Dearle, designer
Britain, 1860 - 1932
Rose and Lily c.1900, London
woven silk and wool, silk and
cotton fringe
229 x 180cm (display)
Gift of Jenny Legoe through
the Art Gallery of South Australia
Foundation 2003
Art Gallery of South Australia,
Adelaide

William Morris Revisited (2000) has elements of the *Rose and Lily* silk and wool curtains that belong to the Art Gallery collection. The lustre of the woven silk is truly incredible and the colours have certainly stood the test of time.

The centre block is adapted from the *Apple* pattern, which was designed in 1895 by John Henry Dearle. Dearle became one of Morris & Co.'s chief designers and after Morris' death became Art Director of The Firm. Dearle's prominence is evident in many textiles, embroideries, tapestries and wallpapers. I adore the large acanthus leaves which are so often a major part in Morris & Co. designs.

Rose, 1883.
Printed chintz used as a cover for
the Kelmscott Chaucer on vellum,
owned by Sidney Cockerell 1896.
Christies Art Library

Coffee with William Morris (2003) was designed while
drinking from a Morris coffee mug on the afternoon of
Christmas Day 2002. The quilt includes elements of the
design on the coffee mug and of the *Rose* wallpaper and chintz
designed by Morris in 1883. It is recorded that Morris was
influenced by a sixteenth century Venetian silk and gold
brocade when he was designing the *Rose* pattern.

My birds sit on the rose stems as in the original piece but
I have arranged them in a different setting. The rose is a
dominant feature and I found that element wonderful to work
with, as was the small three leaf motif above the roses.

Morris & Company, London
Britain, 1861 - 1940
William Morris, designer
Britain, 1834 - 1896
Peacock and Dragon c.1910,
London
woven wool, wool fringe
240 x 167cm
Gift of Mr & Mrs Jock Gosse
1993
Art Gallery of South Australia,
Adelaide

Medieval Morris (2004) was inspired by the woven *Peacock and Dragon* silk and wool curtains from 1881. The curtains that hang in the gallery look incredibly heavy and the texture of the woven wool is screaming out to be touched – only wish I could! I think that the dragons and peacocks are one of the closest links to the Gothic period that Morris so loved.

The upper and lower row of the quilt is based on the *St. James* wallpaper, which was a Royal commission that Morris undertook to redecorate sections of St James' Palace in 1881.

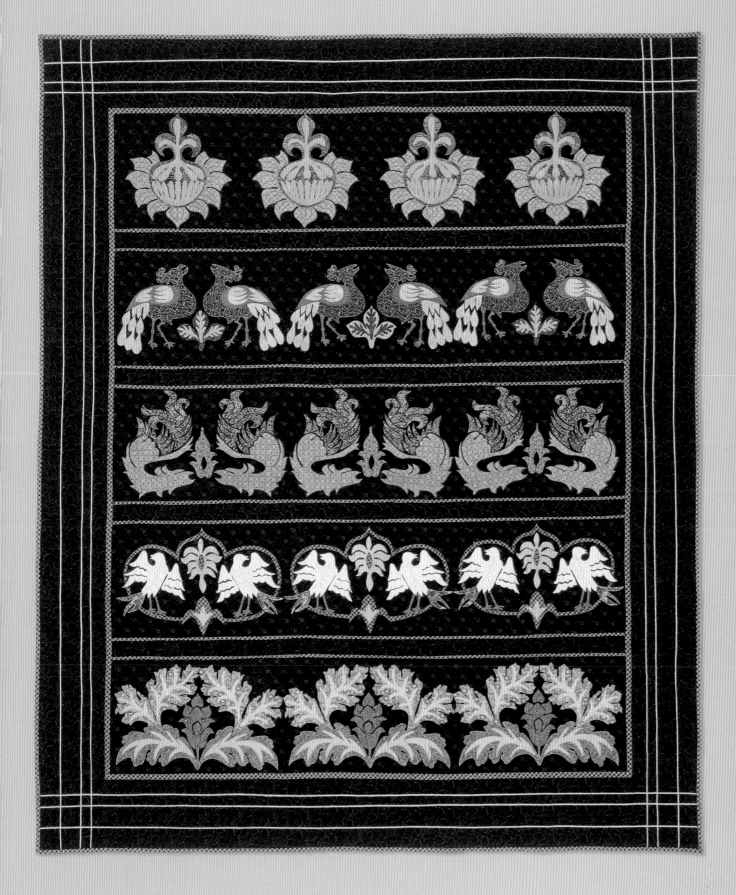

Morris & Company, London
Britain, 1861 - 1940
attributed to May Morris,
designer Britain, 1862 - 1938
Welcome maids of honour
firescreen
c.1900, embroidered Adelaide.
Silk embroidery on silk,
plexiglass, carved oak frame
111 x 65.8 x 42cm
Morris and Company Seminar Fund
Morgan Thomas Bequest Fund
South Australian Government
Grant 1997
Art Gallery of South Australia,
Adelaide

William Morris Floral Sampler (2004) has elements from several wallpaper and fabric designs. This is probably the first time I had the confidence to really start extending Morris' motifs. The original designs include *Cross Twigs (1898)*, *Flower pots (1883)*, *Golden Bough (1888)*, *Crown Imperial (1876)*, *St James (1881)*, *Rose and Lily* and an embroidered firescreen designed by May Morris in the mid 1890s.

The layout of thirteen blocks set on point came to me while walking along a suburban street in Adelaide. A pressed metal shop front had the same configuration complete with scrolls. So the architectural influence was starting to creep into my patterns.

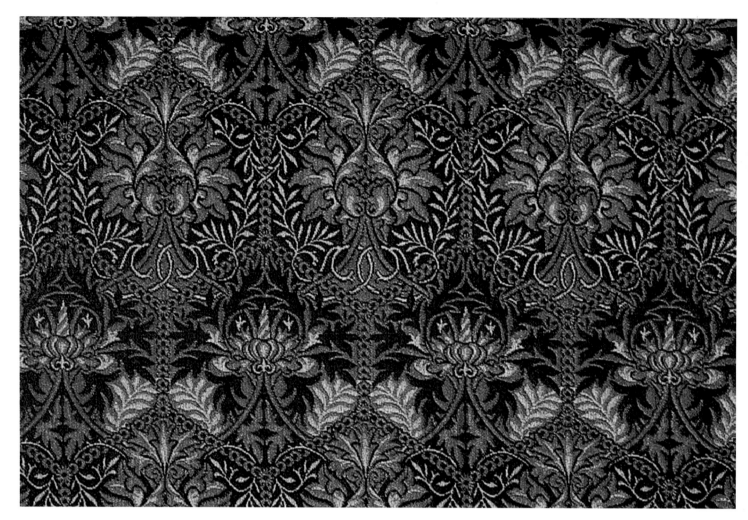

Honeycomb, 1876. Designed by William Morris for both fabric and 3-ply carpeting.

My Renaissance (2006). I have come to appreciate Morris' eye for design. It is recorded that as well as the influence of Medieval art and the Gothic period, he was also inspired by ancient Italian brocades of which he purchased many.

I too began exploring this period and this is the result. Some have called my quilt a '*William Morris*' one, but that is far from true as there is not one motif of Morris' that I used. I was very thrilled to receive the Viewers Choice award for this quilt at the 2006 Quilters Guild of South Australia exhibition – something that I will treasure. Judgement from peers is definitely humbling.

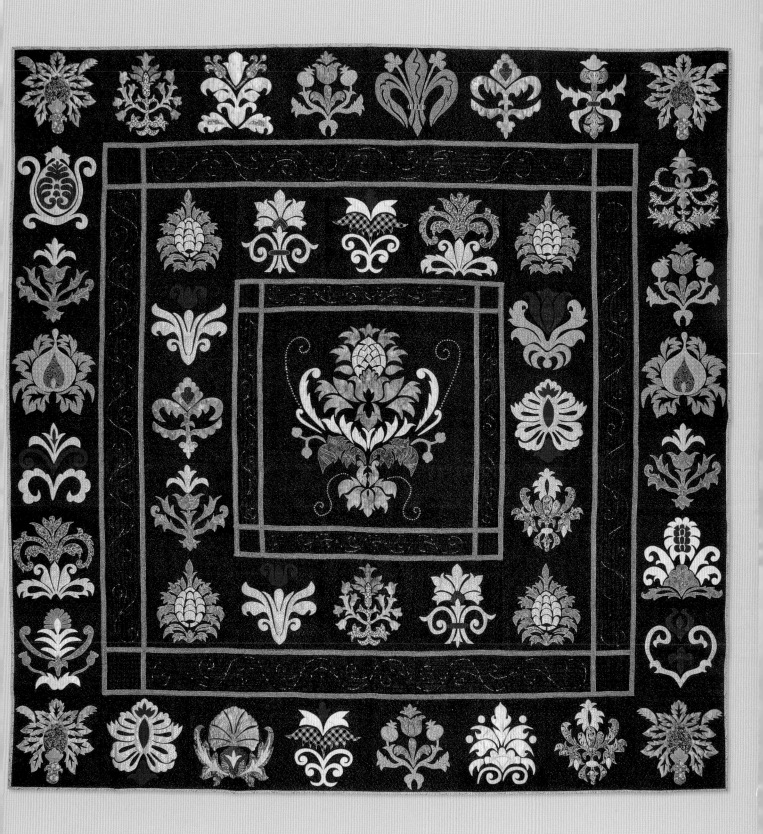

Appliqué projects

Kelmscott Manor was built in the village of Kelmscott on the edge of the Thames in 1570 with an additional wing added in 1665. Morris leased the house in 1871 when his daughters Jenny and May were aged ten and nine. In William Morris' bedroom, the 17th century carved oak bed has a coverlet which was embroidered by his wife Jane. The design has natural flower sprays and a quotation from Morris' poem 'A Garden by the Sea,' taken from his epic work 'The Life and Death of Jason' (1867). She signed it *'Si je puis. Jane Morris. Kelmscott'*.

I have not yet visited Kelmscott Manor and only had a small photo to guide me, so I used motifs from the *Daisy* tile and wallpaper design and the *Celandine* wallpaper to complete the designs for the blocks.

William Morris' bedroom at Kelmscott Manor.

Morris wrote the poem for the embroidered valance that was designed and embroidered by May and some of her friends in 1891.

'For the Bed at Kelmscott',
by William Morris

The wind's on the wold
And the night is a-cold,
And Thames runs chill
Twixt mead and hill,
But kind and dear
Is the old house here,
And my heart is warm
Midst winter's harm.
Rest then and rest,
And think of the best
Twixt summer and spring
When all birds sing
In the town of the tree,
As ye lie in me
And scarce dare move
Lest earth and its love
Should fade away
Ere the full of the day.

Morris & Company, London
Britain, 1861 - 1940
William Morris, designer
Britain, 1834 - 1896
Bird curtain
c.1912, London
woven wool
268 x 72cm
Gift of Tom and Indika Giles 1993
Art Gallery of South Australia, Adelaide

This wall hanging was inspired by William Morris' *Bird*, which he designed in 1878. Morris took inspiration from historical sources and the bird design was adapted from Italian woven silks of the 16th and 17th centuries, which are now in the collection of the Victoria & Albert Museum in London. Woven Bird curtains and an upholstered adjustable-back chair are in the collection of the Art Gallery of South Australia and are a fine example of Morris' woven wool textiles. Morris used forty-four feet of this textile in the drawing room of Kelmscott House. His daughter May described it as *'intimate and friendly …the most adaptable to the needs of everyday life… it suggests not the wealth of the millionaire but the modest competence of a middle class merchant who lives… with the few beautiful things he has collected slowly and carefully'.*

Morris & Company, London
Britain, 1861 - 1940
May Morris, designer
Britain, 1862 - 1938
Erlistoun Mitchell, embroiderer
Australia, 1868 - 1913
Poppy table cover
c.1900, embroidered Adelaide.
Silk embroidery on linen,
silk, silk fringe
107 x 107cm
Gift of Joanna Simpson 1988
Art Gallery of South Australia,
Adelaide

Textiles of the Arts and Crafts Movement are inspirational. Some of the most significant designers of the last 150 years belonged to this period and their legacy is endless. Quilters have used poppies on their quilts for generations. I found them in several embroideries designed by May Morris and find them uplifting. The central panel was inspired by a firescreen made by Morris & Co. c.1880 and the poppy trailing border, from an embroidered table cover, c.1900 designed by May Morris and embroidered in Adelaide, South Australia.

Morris & Company, London
Britain, 1861 - 1940
attributed to May Morris,
designer.
Britain, 1862 - 1938
Tudor rose cushion
designed c.1892
Silk embroidery
7.7 x 50 x 50cm
Private Collection

The Tudor rose takes it name from the Tudor family of Britain and is usually depicted as a white and red double rose. This design from 1892 is attributed to Morris' daughter May. She took a great interest in her father's business and in 1885 became the director of the embroidery section both designing and embroidering until 1922. I find this design lends itself more towards Morris' Sunflower pattern in style and colour.

Detail of watercolour design for **Little Flower** carpet c.1880. Designed by William Morris. Drawings like this were often sent to clients.

Morris Magic was inspired by a working drawing that Morris produced for an embroidery panel (date unknown). Morris took a keen interest in embroidery and was instrumental in the development of Leek School of Embroidery and was one of the first designers when the Royal School of Needlework was founded in 1872 *'to restore ornamental needlework for secular places to the high place it once held among the decorative arts.'* His artwork was often symmetrical and quartered and frequently used for repeat patterns on ceilings, carpets and wallpapers reflecting nature and the flowers that he loved. Designs can be both delicate and dense with vines and leaves intertwining the patterns. Morris' love of ornament and design diversified later in life with the development of Kelmscott Press where Morris reproduced books reflecting the calligraphy of the Middle Ages that he admired so much.

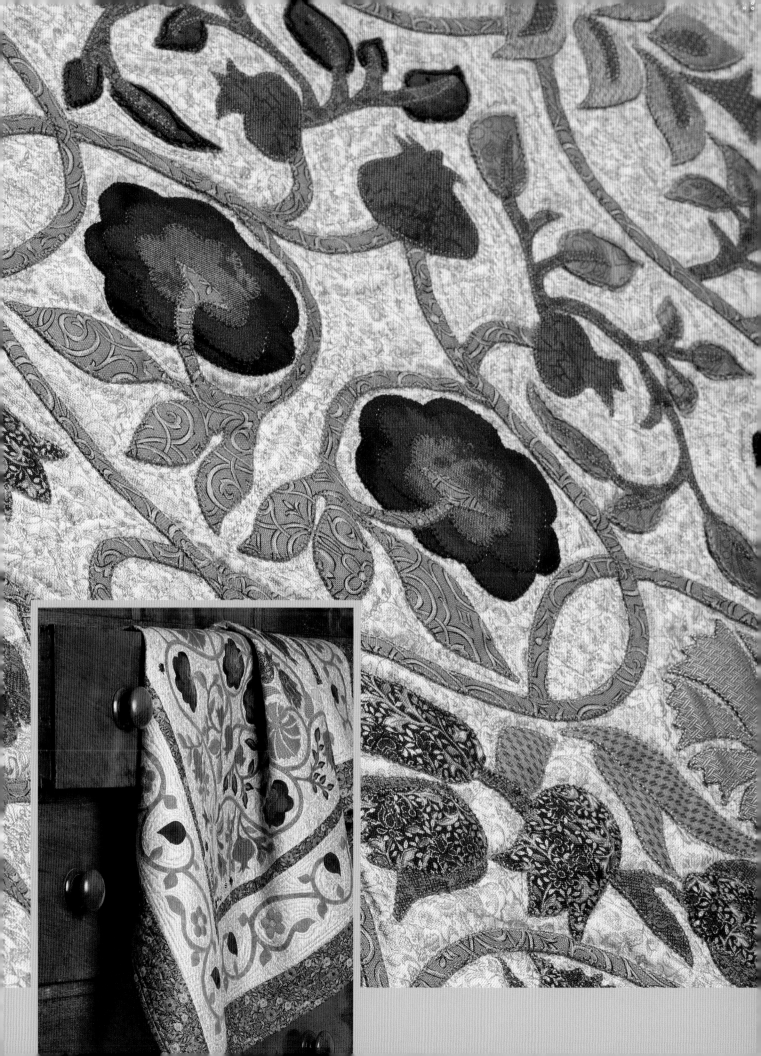

Clients in South Australia were so significant that some samples were named in their honour. Thirty six furnishing fabrics and twenty wallpapers have so far been identified in Adelaide and they include a *'Small Barr'* carpet and two embroideries named *Adelaide* and *Australia*. The Barr Smith family in particular were one of the biggest international clients of Morris & Co. and the Barr Smith women purchased numerous embroidery designs.

This sampler reflects elements from these textiles and includes the corner detail of a table cover and elements of a fire screen, both embroidered in the late 1800s in South Australia.

Morris & Company, London
Britain, 1861 - 1940
attributed to May Morris, designer
Britain, 1862 - 1938
Daughter of Frank and Annie Rymill, embroiderer
Australia
Small anemone table cover
c.1900, Adelaide
silk embroidery on silk
120.8 x 120.8cm
Morgan Thomas Bequest Fund 1993
Art Gallery of South Australia, Adelaide

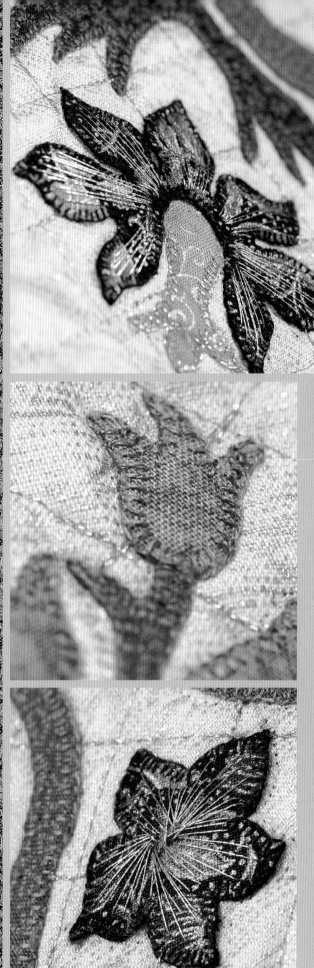

"History has remembered the kings and warriors, because they destroyed;
art has remembered the people, because they created."
William Morris

Kelmscott

This is my interpretation of the coverlet that Morris' wife Jane embroidered for the four poster oak bed at Kelmscott Manor. The knot borders are made using fusible appliqué paper rather than making yards and yards of bias strips. I used a decorative overlock stitch to machine over the knot border making sure it covered both sides. You could try using a feather stitch or herringbone stitch on your machine. Should you prefer to appliqué bias strips, you will need to mark the positions on your quilt before application. The flowers and birds lend themselves to fabrics that reflect nature just as Morris would have done. While some flowers on different blocks may look the same colour, I have made subtle changes by using a similar colour, but a different print. Most of the appliqué is worked by machine, only the bell flowers are outlined by hand in chain stitch using a variegated thread. The individual designs on the blocks could be used to create different size quilts or cushions.

Requirements

Quilt fabrics 44" (112cm) wide

6yd 21 1/4" (6m) cream cotton with metallic gold print (quilt blocks)

23 1/2" (60cm) dark brown cotton with metallic gold print (binding)

6yd (5.5m) light hazelnut cotton print (backing, hanging sleeve)

Appliqué fabrics

Across the fabric width
1yd 14 1/2" (1.2m) dark brown cotton with gold print (knot border)

Fat quarter cotton prints in shades of
Antique blue
Antique gold
Antique white
Burgundy
Coral
Cornflower blue
Garnet
Hazelnut
Mauve
Pink
Wheat
10 - 12 shades of green

Supplies

4yd 14 1/2" x 35 1/2" wide (4m x 90cm) fusible appliqué paper

2yd 22 1/2" (2.4m) square of cotton batting

No. 8 crewel needle

Sharp HB pencil

Threads

Machine rayon embroidery threads
Colours to complement appliqué fabrics

Machine sewing threads
Beige or grey (piecing and bobbin thread for quilting)
Light gold (quilting)
Monofilament

Stranded embroidery cotton
Colours to complement mauve fabrics

STITCHES AND TECHNIQUES USED

CHAIN STITCH
FUSIBLE APPLIQUÉ
FREE MOTION QUILTING
MACHINE BLANKET STITCH
MACHINE GUIDED QUILTING
MACHINE OVERLOCK STITCH
PIECING BY MACHINE

The quilt measures 85" (216cm) square.

Cutting out

Launder all fabrics before cutting out to prevent shrinkage after the quilt is constructed.

Cream cotton with gold print

Blocks
Cut forty one, each 12 1/2" (32cm) square

Setting triangles
Cut four, each 18 1/4" (46.5cm) square. Cut each into four quarter-square triangles

Corner triangles
Cut two, each 9 3/8" (24cm) square. Cut each into two half-square triangles

Dark brown cotton with gold print

Binding
Cut nine, each 2 1/2" (6.5cm) across the fabric width

Light hazelnut cotton print

Backing
Cut two, each 2yd 16 5/8" (225cm) across the fabric width

Hanging sleeve
Cut two, each 12" x 43" wide (30cm x 108cm)

Preparation for appliqué

See pattern sheet 3, side 2 and sheet 4, side 1 for the appliqué designs.

Following the instructions on pages 81 and 82, trace the appliqué shapes onto separate pieces of appliqué paper. Number the pattern pieces to assist with placement of designs and to keep track of what you have traced. Referring to the layout diagram in the pattern sheet, trace the shapes for each block the required number of times.

Block 1 - 9 times
Block 2 - 6 times
Block 3 - 4 times
Block 4 - 4 times
Block 5 - 6 times
Block 6 - 4 times
Block 7 - 4 times
Block 8 - 4 times

Using the quilt assembly diagram as a guide, trace the shapes for each bird the number of times indicated on the pattern sheet following the instructions on page 81 to achieve correct orientation.

Working with one motif at a time, fuse the appliqué shapes to the wrong side of the appropriate fabrics and cut out. Take note that the same motif is worked in several colour variations to achieve a more 'natural' result.

Trace the shape for the knot border fifty times, all facing in the same direction as indicated in the diagram below. Fuse to the wrong side of the dark brown cotton print.

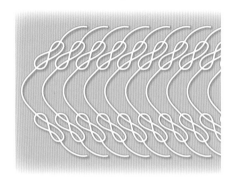

Preparing the quilt blocks and borders
Fold each block into quarters and finger press the foldlines to mark the centre. Use this as a guide when positioning the appliqué pieces. Alternatively transfer the design outlines onto the blocks following the instructions on page 80.

Cutting layout
Cream cotton gold print
1. Block
2. Setting triangle
3. Corner triangle

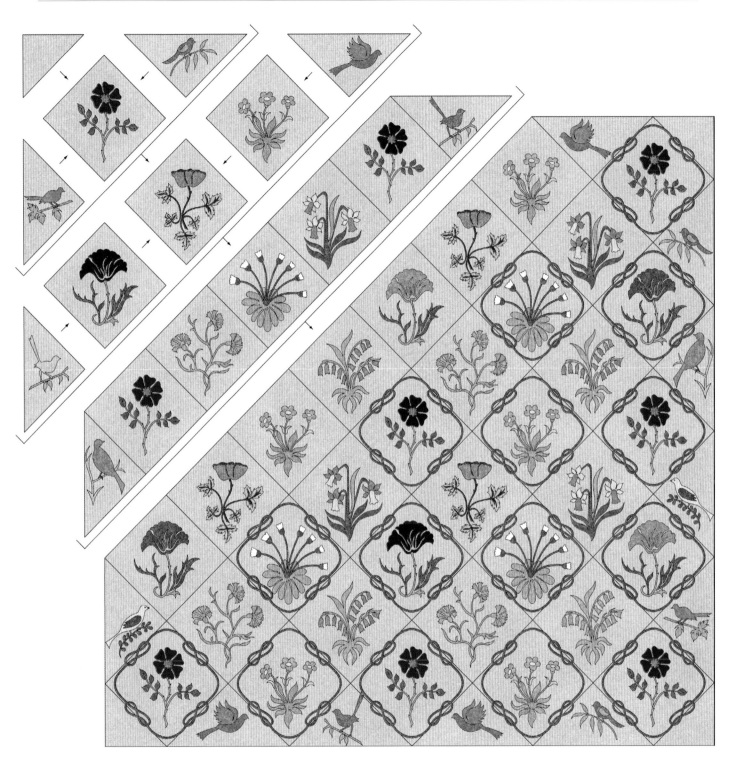

QUILT ASSEMBLY DIAGRAM - COLOUR KEY

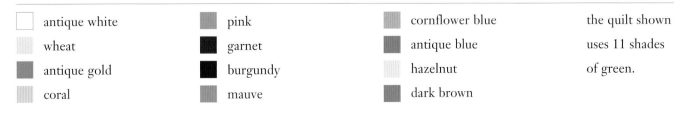

antique white	pink	cornflower blue	the quilt shown
wheat	garnet	antique blue	uses 11 shades
antique gold	burgundy	hazelnut	of green.
coral	mauve	dark brown	

Appliqué

The applique motifs on the blocks and triangles are completed and the quilt top is pieced before the knot borders are worked. See pages 82 - 85 for general and step-by-step instructions.

Quilt blocks and triangles

Using the photographs and quilt assembly diagrams as a guide for colour placement, position the appliqué shapes. Overlap the shapes as indicated by the dotted lines on the pattern sheet. Fuse the pieces in place as you go.

Using two strands of matching stranded cotton, work chain stitch around the bellflowers. Work machine blanket stitch around all remaining appliqué pieces using matching machine embroidery thread on top and neutral thread on the bobbin.

If you choose to work the blanket stitch by hand, use one strand of matching stranded cotton.

Knot border

Appliqué the borders around the flowers in alternate rows following the step-by-step instructions on the facing page.

Piecing and quilting

All piecing is worked using a ¹/4" (5mm) seam allowance. See pages 86 - 100 for the step-by-step instructions.

Piecing

Referring to the quilt assembly diagram, join the blocks and triangles into diagonal rows as shown. Press the seams in alternate rows in the opposite directions. Handle the triangles carefully when you stitch as the edges cut on the bias will stretch and distort easily. Join the pieced strips, making sure the seams are aligned and the seam allowances are pressed in opposite directions.

Preparing the backing

Cut the backing fabric to size. Trim the selvedges and join the pieces along the length. Press the seam open.

Layering

Layer the backing, batting and quilt top and baste them together using your chosen method, following the instructions on page 89.

Quilting

All quilting is worked using matching machine quilting thread on the bobbin.

Free motion quilt along both sides of the knot borders and around the outline of the appliqué shapes using monofilament thread on top. Change the top thread to matching quilting thread and quilt the background as you choose.

The quilt shown is quilted in the following patterns.

Fill the background inside the knot borders with free motion echo quilting.

Mark and stitch a 10 1/4" (26cm) diameter circle around the flower motifs without borders. Stitch a second circle inside the first and fill it with stipple quilting.

Work a single row of echo quilting around each bird motif and a three leaf pattern at each corner before filling the remainder of the background with a paisley pattern.

Finishing

All seam allowances are 1/4" (5mm).

Block, square and finish the quilt following the instructions on pages 100 - 105.

Paisley quilt pattern

KNOT BORDERS

Each knot border is cut as two halves with the overlap at the upper and lower edge. The borders are placed around the flowers in alternate rows.

Cut out all the pieces. For stability, cut the fabric inside the knots before cutting the narrow sections. Refer to the layout diagram for placement of the knot borders. Use an open-toe presser foot and test your chosen stitch width on a spare piece of fabric before you begin.

We used contrasting thread for photographic purposes.

1. Position and fuse two border halves into place around a flower motif, overlapping the ends slightly at the upper and lower edges.

2. Set your machine to a wide overlock stitch or similar. Begin stitching, ensuring the stitch covers the full width of the appliqué.

3. Continue around each knot, stitching over previous stitching.

If you choose to work the knot border by hand, work closed feather stitch following the instructions on page 116.

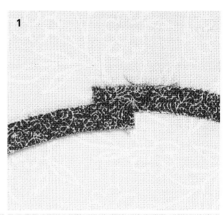

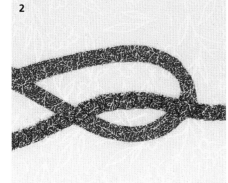

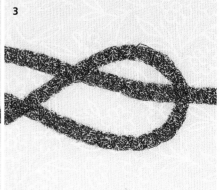

"The true secret of happiness lies in taking a genuine interest
in all the details of daily life." *William Morris*

Bird

Birds often appear in Morris designs and I enjoy their presence! The original *Bird* curtain has a dense and almost quilted surface texture consisting of layers of woven wool. If one looks carefully you will find a sprinkling of gold in the midst of the dominant blue. This small hanging reflects this with a background of blue fabric and the use of many small prints accentuated with metallic gold on the birds and sunflower. Smaller flowers have been 'fussy cut' as was popular in the 19th century when broderie perse was widely used. To do this you need a fabric with motifs of flowers that can be cut out and appliquéd as a whole.

Requirements

Quilt fabrics 44" (112cm) wide

2yd 26¹/2" (2.5m) antique blue cotton print

8" (20cm) black cotton with metallic gold print (sashing)

Appliqué fabrics

Across the fabric width
24" (60cm) blue and white floral print (leaf border and foliage)

Fat eighths cotton prints
Black with red floral
Copper wash
Coral-copper wash
Dark navy floral
Hazelnut
Light coral wash
Metallic gold
Multi coloured
Red with gold floral

Supplies

60" x 35¹/2" wide (1.5m x 90cm) fusible appliqué paper

44" x 32" wide (110cm x 80cm) piece of cotton batting

No. 9 crewel needle

Sharp HB pencil

Threads

Machine sewing threads
Dusty blue (quilting)
Beige or grey cotton (piecing and bobbin thread for machine appliqué)
Monofilament (quilting)

Stranded rayon
Colours to complement appliqué fabrics.

Cutting out

Launder all fabrics before cutting out to prevent shrinkage after the quilt is constructed.

Antique blue cotton print

Centre panel
Cut one 16¹/2" x 28¹/2" wide (42cm x 72cm)

Appliqué border
Cut four, each 5" (13cm) across the fabric width

Binding
Cut four, each 2¹/2" (6.5cm) across the fabric width

Backing
Cut one 32" x 44" wide (82cm x 112cm)

Hanging sleeves
Cut two, each 5" x 29" wide (13cm x 73cm)

Black with gold cotton print

Sashing
Cut four, each 1¹/2" (3.5cm) across the fabric width

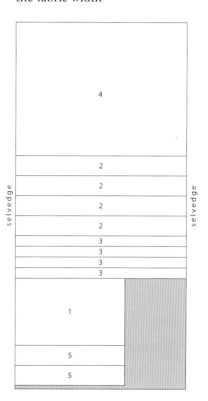

Cutting layout

Antique blue cotton print
1. Centre panel
2. Appliqué border
3. Binding
4. Backing
5. Hanging sleeve

The wall hanging measures 27¹/2" x 39¹/2" long (70cm x 101cm).

Preparation for appliqué

See pattern sheet 1, side 1 for the appliqué design. Refer to the general instructions on pages 81 and 82.

Trace the appliqué pieces onto separate pieces of appliqué paper. Trace the leaf for the border thirty-two times.

Referring to the quilt assembly diagram for colour placement, fuse the appliqué pieces to the wrong side of the appropriate fabrics and cut out along the marked lines. Number and group the pieces and set aside.

Preparing the quilt blocks and borders

Fold the centre panel into quarters and finger press the foldlines to mark the centre. Use this as a guide when positioning the appliqué pieces.

Alternatively transfer the design outlines onto the centre panel following the instructions on page 80.

Appliqué

See pages 82 - 85 for general and step-by-step instructions.

Centre panel

Position the appliqué motifs as shown in the quilt assembly diagram, overlapping the shapes as indicated by the dotted lines on the pattern sheet. Fuse the pieces in place as you work.

Using two strands of matching stranded rayon, work slanted blanket stitch around all appliqué pieces, referring to the instructions on page 85.

Leaf border

Positioning the leaves in a zigzag pattern, work the outer border in the same manner after the quilt top is pieced.

Embroidery

Using brown embroidery thread, outline the eye of the large birds in back stitch. Work the pupil in satin stitch and outline in back stitch.

Piecing and quilting

All piecing is worked using a 1/4" (5mm) seam allowance.

Piecing the sashing and borders

Referring to the quilt assembly diagram, measure and piece the sashing to the centre panel following the instructions on pages 87 and 88. Repeat for the borders.

Layering

Layer the backing, batting and quilt top and baste them together following the instructions on page 89.

Quilting

All quilting is worked using matching machine quilting thread on the bobbin.

Using matching machine quilting thread on top, stitch in the ditch along each side of the sashing strips to stabilise the quilt. Change to monofilament thread and free motion quilt along the edge of the appliqué shapes. Stitch a tight spiral in the centre of each small red flower.

Using matching quilting thread, stipple quilt across all the blank spaces of the centre panel and border, incorporating the centre veins of the leaves.

Finishing

All seam allowances are 1/4" (5mm).

Block, square and finish the quilt following the instructions on pages 100 - 105.

STITCHES AND TECHNIQUES USED

BACK STITCH

FREE MOTION QUILTING

FUSIBLE APPLIQUÉ

MACHINE BLANKET STITCH

MACHINE GUIDED QUILTING

PIECING BY MACHINE

SATIN STITCH

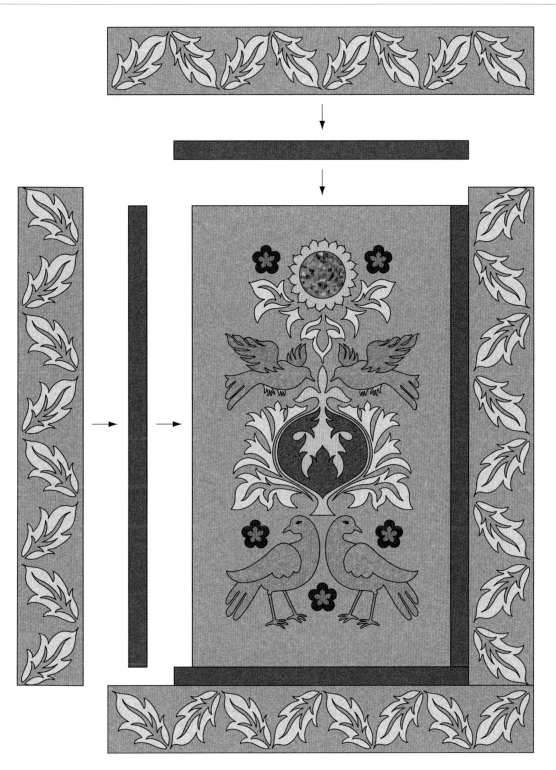

QUILT ASSEMBLY DIAGRAM – COLOUR KEY

metallic gold	hazelnut	pale blue floral
lt coral	red-gold	dk navy
coral-copper	multi coloured	
copper	black-red	

"Give me love and work – these two only."
William Morris

The quilt measures 72" (183cm) square.

Friends

Most of the blocks around the border of this quilt are Morris designs but I have also used bird and flower patterns from Charles Voysey, Walter Crane and Charles Harrison Townsend. To complement the sashing I applied a decorative braid over the seams after the quilting was complete. The individual designs lend themselves to a number of different projects. The centre panel would make a wonderful firescreen on its own while the border blocks are perfect for cushions or joined together four across and five deep for a fabulous quilt top.

Blocks 1 and 11. **Spring Thicket**, William Morris 1894

Requirements

Quilt fabrics 44" (112cm) wide

4yd 5 5/8" (3.8m) cream on cream cotton print (centre panel, blocks, border)

1yd 12" (120cm) feature cotton print (sashing, binding)

5yd 17" (5m) cream and tan cotton print (backing, hanging sleeve)

Appliqué fabrics

Across the fabric width

12" (30cm) burgundy cotton print (poppies)

20" (50cm) each, two shades of soft green cotton print (stems and foliage)

20" (50cm) each, two shades of darker green cotton print (foliage)

Fat quarters and fat eighths cotton prints in shades of

Antique gold
Burnt olive
Copper
Coral
Dark olive green with pink
Garnet
Light blue-green
Light hazelnut
Mauve

Mocha brown
Salmon
Very dark green

Supplies

17yd 18" x 1/2" wide (16m x 12mm) decorative braid complementing feature cotton print

4yd 13 1/2" x 35 1/2" wide (4m x 90cm) fusible applique paper

80" (2m) square of cotton batting

Tracing paper

Fine black pen

Sharp HB pencil

Threads

Machine rayon embroidery threads
Colours to complement fabrics (appliqué)
Cream (quilting)

Machine sewing threads
Beige or grey (piecing and bobbin thread for machine appliqué)
Cream (quilting)
Monofilament (quilting)

Block 3. **Rose**, William Morris 1883

> **STITCHES AND TECHNIQUES USED**
> FREE MOTION QUILTING · FUSIBLE APPLIQUÉ
> MACHINE BLANKET STITCH · MACHINE GUIDED QUILTING
> PIECING BY MACHINE

Block 2. **Autumn Flowers**, William Morris 1888

Cutting out

Launder all fabrics before cutting out to prevent shrinkage after the quilt is constructed.

Cream on cream cotton print

Centre panel

Cut one 26$\frac{1}{2}$ (67cm) square

Poppy borders

Cut four, each 6$\frac{1}{2}$" (16cm) across the fabric width

Outer border blocks

Cut twenty, each 12$\frac{1}{2}$ (31cm) square

Feature cotton print

Sashing

Cut eight, each 3" (7.5cm) wide across the fabric width

Binding

Cut seven, each 2$\frac{1}{2}$ (6.5cm) wide across the fabric width

Cream and tan cotton print

Backing

Cut two, each 2yd 6$\frac{3}{4}$ (2m) across the fabric width

Hanging sleeve

Cut two, each 12" x 36$\frac{1}{2}$ wide (30cm x 90cm)

Cutting layout

Cream on cream cotton print

1. Centre panel
2. Poppy borders
3. Outer border blocks

Preparation for appliqué

See pattern sheet 1, side 2, sheet 2, sides 1 and 2 and sheet 3, side 1 for the appliqué designs.
Refer to the general instructions on pages 81 and 82.

Tape pieces of tracing paper together to make a 26$\frac{1}{2}$" (67.5cm) square. Rule a line along the centre. Aligning the ruled line with the placement guides on the design, trace one half of the centre design. Lift the tracing and turn it to the other side. Reposition the tracing over the design, aligning the centre line and trace the second half. Trace the block motifs in a similar manner onto separate pieces of tracing paper.

Trace the appliqué shapes onto separate pieces of appliqué paper using the pencil. Trace the pieces for the poppy border as indicated on the pattern sheet.

Using the photographs and quilt assembly diagram as a guide, fuse the appliqué shapes to the wrong side of the appropriate fabric pieces and cut out along the marked lines. Number and group the pieces and set aside.

Preparing the quilt blocks and borders

Fold each block into quarters and finger press the foldlines to mark the centre. Use this as a guide when positioning the appliqué pieces. Alternatively, transfer the design outlines onto the blocks following the instructions on page 80.

Appliqué

See pages 82 - 85 for step-by-step and general instructions.

Order of work

Centre and outer border blocks

Using the photographs as a guide, position the appliqué pieces, over-lapping the shapes as indicated by the dotted lines on the pattern sheet. Fuse the pieces in place as you go.

Work machine blanket stitch around all edges of the appliqué pieces using matching machine embroidery thread on top and neutral thread on the bobbin.

Alternatively, work the blanket stitch by hand, using one strand of matching cotton.

Poppy border

To allow the shapes at the corners to cover the seams, work the appliqué on the poppy border in a similar manner after the quilt is pieced, centering the designs along the length of the border pieces.

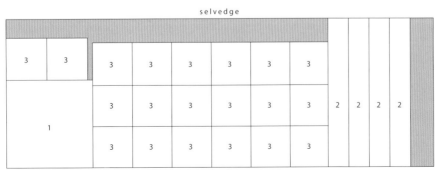

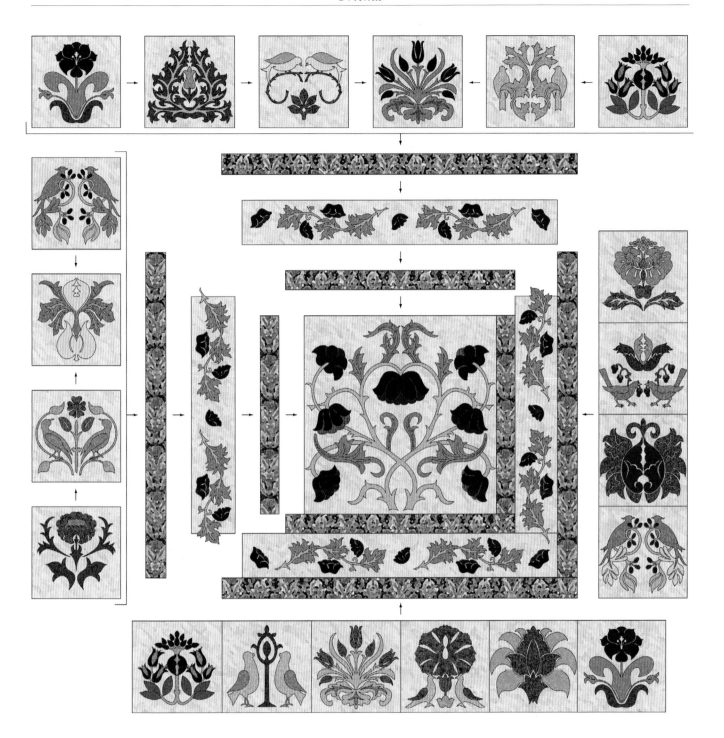

QUILT ASSEMBLY DIAGRAM - COLOUR KEY

- copper
- garnet
- burgundy
- mocha brown
- hazelnut

- salmon
- coral
- antique gold
- burnt olive
- dk olive-pink

- vy dk green
- dk green
- green
- fern green
- blue-green

- lt blue-green
- mauve

Blocks 4 and 14. **Tulip,** William Morris 1875

Block 5. **Wallpaper and textile design,**
Charles Voysey 1909

Blocks 6 and 16. **Omar,** C. Harrison Townsend 1896

Block 7. **Tulip and Rose,** William Morris 1876

Block 8. **Strawberry Thief,** William Morris 1883

Block 9. **Honeycomb,** William Morris 1876

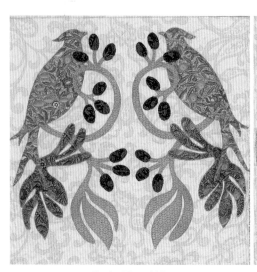

Blocks 10 and 20.
Wallpaper design, Charles Voysey 1909

Block 12. **Indian,** William Morris 1868 - 70

Block 13. **Saladin,** Charles Voysey 1897

Block 15, Detail, **Brer Rabbit**, William Morris 1882

Block 17, **Myrtle**, William Morris 1899

Block 18, Stencil design, Walter Crane 1890s

Piecing and quilting

All piecing is worked using a 1/4" (5mm) seam allowance.

Preparing the sashing strips

Trim two pieces to measure 26 1/2" (67cm) long

Trim two pieces to measure 31 1/2" (80cm) long

Trim two pieces to measure 43 1/2" (110.5cm) long

Use the two pieces that were cut from the shortest strips and join each to the remaining full length strips.

Trim the extended strips to measure 48 1/2" (123cm) long.

Piecing the sashing and borders

Referring to the quilt assembly diagram, join two rows of four blocks for each outer side border. Join two rows of six blocks for the upper and lower outer borders.

Piece the sashing strips and poppy borders around the centre panel. If necessary ease the edges off the appliquéd pieces to fit the sashing strips to ensure an exact fit for the block borders. When attaching the upper and lower block borders, ensure the stitchlines at the outer blocks are aligned with the stitchline on the side border.

Work the appliqué on the poppy border, varying the position of the poppies along each side.

Preparing the backing

Cut the backing fabric to size. Trim the selvedges and join the pieces along the length. Press the seam open.

Layering

Layer the backing, batting and quilt top and baste them together follow-ing the instructions on page 89.

Quilting

All quilting is worked using matching machine quilting thread on the bobbin.

Using matching quilting thread on top, stitch in the ditch along the seamlines to stabilise the quilt. Change to monofilament thread and free motion quilt along the edge of the appliqué shapes. Replace the quilting thread on top and quilt the background as you choose.

The quilt shown is worked with the following quilt patterns.

Echo quilt the background of the centre panel and the border blocks. Work the quilting on the poppy border with a scrolling pattern. Quilt the sashing with a scallop pattern on the inner border and cross hatching on the outer.

Braid

Using a wide zigzag stitch and matching thread, stitch the decorative braid in place, covering the stitchlines of the sashing.

Finishing

All seam allowances are 1/4" (5mm). Block, square and finish the quilt following the instructions on pages 100 - 105.

Block 19. **Artichoke**, William Morris 1875 - 80

"The past is not dead, it is living in us, and will be alive in the future which we are now helping to make." *William Morris*

The cushion measures 20" (50cm) square.

Tudor Rose

The bold colours used for the large tudor rose in the centre of the cushion reflect the red and orange tones of the original silk embroidery, offset against a light coloured print to accentuate the small stamens of the flower. The shapes are outlined by hand using two strands of thread for the blanket stitch to emphasize and add texture to the design lines and some shapes are outlined using a variegated thread for added detail.

Requirements

Cushion fabric

24" x 44" wide (60cm x 112cm) beige with grey-green print cotton

Appliqué fabrics

Fat quarter cotton prints in shades of
Olive green
Soft grey-green
Burnt orange
Wheat
Garnet
Burgundy with orange

Supplies

20" x 35 1/2" wide (50cm x 90cm) fusible appliqué paper

20" (50cm) cushion insert

16" (40cm) zip

83" (2.1m) rayon flanged cord to complement fabric

No.9 crewel needle

Sharp HB pencil

Threads

Stranded cotton
Colours to complement appliqué fabrics.

Machine sewing thread
Beige

Cutting out

Launder all fabrics before cutting out to prevent shrinkage after the cushion is constructed.

Front
Cut one 20 3/4" (52cm) square

Back
Cut two, each 11" x 20 3/4" wide (28cm x 52cm)

Cutting layout

Beige cotton with grey-green print
1. Front 2. Back

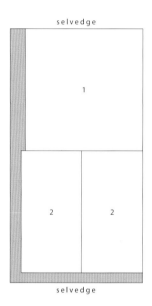

QUILT ASSEMBLY DIAGRAM - COLOUR KEY

wheat

burnt orange

burgundy-orange

garnet

olive green

soft grey-green

Preparation for appliqué

See pattern sheet 1, side 2 for the appliqué design. Refer to the general instructions on pages 81 and 82.

The centre of the design is formed by layering the appliqué shapes. Trace the outline of each layer individually and all other shapes onto separate pieces of appliqué paper.

Preparing the cushion front

Fold the front piece into quarters and finger press the foldlines to mark the centre. Use this as a guide when positioning the appliqué pieces.

Alternatively, transfer the design outlines onto the fabric following the instructions on page 80.

Appliqué

See pages 82 - 85 for step-by-step and general instructions.

Position the appliqué shapes as shown in the assembly diagram, layering the pieces for the rose. Overlap the remaining shapes as indicated by the dotted lines on the pattern sheet. Fuse the pieces in place as you work.

Using two strands of stranded cotton in colours to complement the appliqué fabrics, outline each shape with blanket stitch.

Alternatively, outline the shapes using a machine blanket stitch and matching machine embroidery thread.

Constructing the cushion

Attaching the flanged cord

1. Beginning at the centre on one side of the front, position the flange of the cord inside the seam allowance. Leave a 4" (10cm) tail of cord and pin to the right side of the front around all sides, easing around the corners. Pin and stitch around the cushion as close as possible to the cord *(diag 1)*. Stop stitching 3 1/2" (9cm) from the beginning.

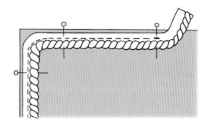

Joining the flanged cord

2. Leaving 4" (10cm) of cord, trim away the excess *(diag 2)*.

Overlap the two ends of the cord. Mark each piece with a pin at the overlap point *(diag 3)*.

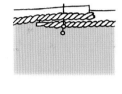

At one end, unpick the thread securing the cord to the flange, back to the pin *(diag 4)*.

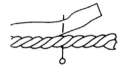

3. Unravel the twists in the free length of cord to separate the segments *(diag 5)*.

Flatten the unravelled segments and curve them towards the edge of the flange. Ensure the segments lie side by side *(diag 6)*.

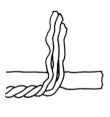

Tack the segments to the edge of the flange.

4. Repeat for the remaining end of the cord, ensuring the segments curve over the reverse side of the flange *(diag 7)*.

5. With the unravelled segments of the cord facing each other, place the two ends of the cord so the twists lie snugly together *(diag 8)*.

Machine stitch the ends together for 1 ⅛" (3cm) along the top of the flange. Trim away the excess flange and cord *(diag 9)*.

6. Pin the joined cord to the fabric and stitch in place *(diag 10)*.

7. Joining the back pieces

Neaten one long side of each back piece with a machine zigzag or overlock stitch. Press under a ⅝" (1.5cm) seam allowance along each neatened edge. Unfold. Matching the pressed foldlines, place the two pieces with right sides together.

At each end, stitch along the foldline for 2cm (5"). Tack along the remainder of the foldline *(diag 11)*. Press the seam open.

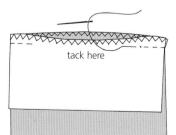

tack here

8. Inserting the zip

Stitch across the top of the zip to hold the two pieces of tape together *(diag 12)*.

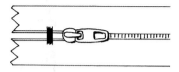

With the right side of the zip facing the wrong side of the cushion back, centre the zip on the tacked section of the seam. Pin and tack in place *(diag 13)*.

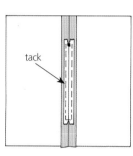

tack

Remove the pins. With the right side facing up, stitch the zip in place, stitching ¼" (6mm) from the seam on both sides and across the end *(diag 14)*.

stitch

Trim the corners in the same manner as the front piece. Remove the tacking and open the zip.

9. Joining the front to the back

With right sides together and matching raw edges, pin and tack the cushion front to the back. The piping is sandwiched between. With the front uppermost, stitch around all sides along the previous stitchline.

Turn the cushion cover through to the right side.

"Not on one strand are all life's jewels strung." *William Morris*

The quilt measures 56"(142cm) square.

Morris Magic

This symmetrical pattern is based on a William Morris sketch of flowers, leaves and intertwining stems. It is necessary to mark this intricate design onto the background fabric to ensure the appliqué motifs and bias binding stems are accurately placed. Despite transferring the design very carefully, I still found the end result slightly off centre. To finish the quilt I decided to add small charms and hand embroidered bees and ladybirds at the corners. The position and number of little 'critters' differs at each corner. When selecting fabrics look for very small prints or even hand dyed cottons. Packs often come in muted shades from light to dark. This works well and is what I used in the red flowers.

Requirements

Quilt fabrics 44" (112cm) wide

1yd 35" (1.8m) cream cotton with metallic gold print (centre panel, appliqué border)

44" (112cm) dark floral cotton print (sashing, outer border, binding)

4yd 6" (3.8m) dark purple floral cotton print (backing, hanging sleeve)

Appliqué fabrics

Across the fabric width

20" (50cm) antique gold cotton print (bias scroll)

8" (20cm) each, three shades of green cotton print

Fat quarter cotton prints

Burgundy

Burnt orange

Dark green and burgundy floral

Dark salmon wash

Wine red with gold

Two shades of garnet

Four shades of blue

Supplies

Gold and silver coloured insect charms

Gold seed beads

Clear silver lined seed beads

2yd 7" x 35 1/2" wide (2m x 90cm) fusible appliqué paper

63" (160cm) square of cotton batting

1/4" (6mm) bias maker

Tracing paper

Chalk pencil

Fine black pen

Sharp HB pencil

Needles

No. 8 crewel

No. 10 crewel

No. 9 milliner's

Threads

Machine rayon embroidery threads
Colours to complement appliqué fabrics.
Antique gold (quilting)

Machine sewing threads
Beige or grey (piecing and bobbin thread for appliqué and quilting)
Monofilament (quilting)

Stranded cotton
Black, red, white, yellow
Two shades of green to match small leaves.

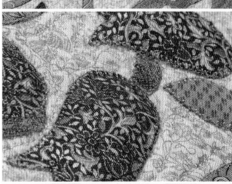
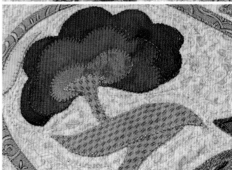

STITCHES AND TECHNIQUES USED

BEADING · BULLION KNOT · CHAIN STITCH · FREE MOTION QUILTING
FUSIBLE APPLIQUÉ · MACHINE BLANKET STITCH
MACHINE GUIDED QUILTING · PIECING BY MACHINE

Cutting out

Launder all fabrics before cutting out to prevent shrinkage after the quilt is constructed.

Cream cotton with metallic gold print

Centre panel
Cut one 40¹/₂" (102cm) square

Appliqué border
Cut five strips, each 5" (12.5cm) across the fabric width

Dark floral cotton print

Sashing
Cut four strips, each 1¹/₄" (3cm) across the fabric width

Outer border
Cut six strips, each 3" (7.5cm) across the fabric width

Binding
Cut six strips, each 2¹/₂" (6.5cm) across the fabric width

Dark purple floral cotton print

Backing
Cut two, each 63" x 31¹/₂" wide (160cm x 80cm)

Hanging sleeve
Cut two, each 10¹/₄" x 28³/₄" wide (26cm x 73cm)

Cutting layout

Cream cotton with metallic gold print
1. Centre panel
2. Appliqué border

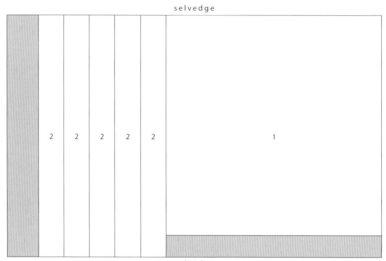

Preparation for appliqué

See pattern sheet 4, side 2 for the appliqué design.
Refer to the general instructions on pages 80 - 82.

Using the pencil, trace the appliqué pieces, four times each onto separate pieces of fusible appliqué paper. Trace the border pieces the number of times indicated on the pattern sheet. Use the photograph and appliqué diagram as a guide for colour placement. Fuse the appliqué pieces to the wrong side of the appropriate fabric pieces and cut out along the marked lines. Number and group the pieces and set aside.

Making bias strips
Following the instructions on pages 64 and 79 prepare a 10yd 34" x ¹/₄" wide (10m x 6mm) bias strip from the antique gold cotton print.

Transferring the design

The design is transferred onto one quarter of the centre panel at a time. Prepare the tracing following steps 1 and 2 on page 80. Fold the centre panel into quarters and finger press the folds to mark the centre. Unfold. Position one quarter of the fabric over the tracing, aligning the centre and foldlines with the centre mark and placement guides. Using the chalk pencil, trace the design outlines onto the first quarter of the fabric, tracing just inside the design lines. Rotate the fabric 90°, re-aligning the placement guides

and repeat for the second quarter. Transfer the design onto the remaining two quarters in the same manner.

Preparing the appliqué border
Cut one border strip in half and join each piece to a full strip.

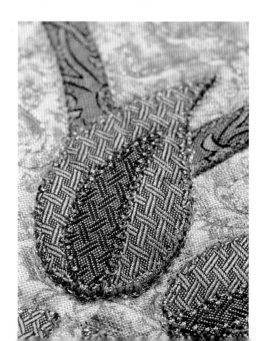

Appliqué diagram – colour key

antique gold	wine red	blue
burnt orange	dk salmon	dk green
garnet	lt cornflower blue	fern green
lt garnet	cornflower blue	dk olive green
burgundy	med cornflower blue	green-burgundy

USING A BIAS MAKER

A bias maker is a small tool through which narrow strips of fabric can be passed to fold the sides evenly to the back. Some bias makers allow you to add fusible tape to the back of the bias strip at the same time. The metal side of the bias maker has a slot where the fabric folds over as it is pulled through and a plastic slot on the top where the fusible tape is pulled though.

Cut the required number of fabric strips twice the finished width.

1. Slide the tip of the fabric strip into the slot and feed it through using a pin.

2. Pull a short length of fabric through the bias maker.

3. With the paper side facing up, feed the fusible tape through the top slot and place the end along the folded bias strip. Fuse in place along short lengths at a time using a warm dry iron.

Alternatively, make and press your bias strip and fuse a narrow strip of fusible appliqué paper to the wrong side.

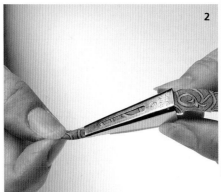

Appliqué

See pages 82 - 85 for step-by-step and general instructions. Take note that the diagram is a quarter of the overall design.

Order of work

Position and fuse each design element on all four quarters of the quilt at a time, finishing with the motifs along the centre lines. The layering of the appliqué pieces is quite intricate because of the intertwining stems. The layering is indicated by the dotted lines on the pattern sheet. Fuse the pieces in place as you work, taking note that subsequent pieces may need to underlap. Add the extra end scroll at each end of the side borders.

Position the appliqué shapes beginning with the red flowers and tiny leaves. Next add the large blue carnations and olive green stems leaving the tips free where the orange pomegranates underlap. Continue to position and layer the motifs and bias stems.

Using two strands of matching stranded cotton, work chain stitch around all the small leaves referring to step 7 on page 85. Work machine blanket stitch around all remaining appliqué pieces using matching machine embroidery thread. Work the appliqué on the border pieces in a similar manner centering the designs along the length of each piece.

If you choose to work the blanket stitch by hand, use one strand of matching stranded cotton.

Piecing and quilting

All piecing is worked using a ¼" (5mm) seam allowance.

Preparing the sashing and borders

Cut two sashing strips in half and join each half to a full length strip. Repeat for the border strips.

Piecing the sashing and borders

Referring to the layout diagram, measure and piece the sashing and borders around the centre panel referring to the assembly diagram and step-by-step instructions on page 87.

If the appliqué borders require adjustment in length, trim evenly from each end to ensure the border design is centred along the edge.

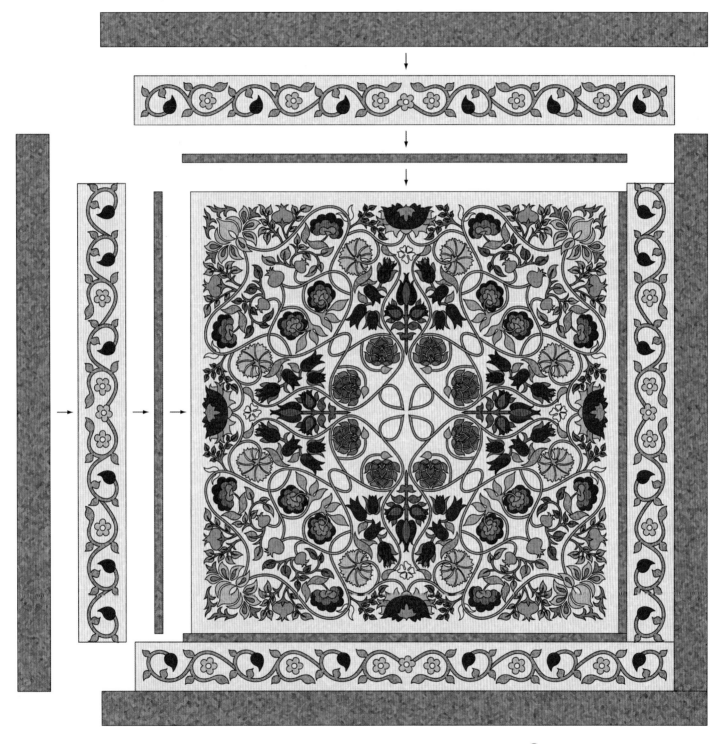

QUILT ASSEMBLY DIAGRAM

Preparing the backing

Cut the backing fabric to size. Trim the selvedges and join the pieces along the length. Press the seam open.

Layering

Layer the backing, batting and quilt top and baste them together using your chosen method, following the instructions on page 89.

Quilting

All quilting is worked using matching machine quilting thread on the bobbin.

Using matching machine quilting thread on top, stitch in the ditch along the seamlines to stabilise the quilt. Change to monofilament thread and free motion quilt along the edge of the appliqué shapes.

Change the top thread to matching quilting thread and quilt the background as you choose.

The quilt shown is quilted in the following patterns.

Work cross hatching in the centre of the quilt panel and in the small ovals within the bias stems.

Cover the background between the outer edge of the centre design and the sashing with a scroll pattern.

Stitch two straight rows along the sashing and the outer row and fill the remaining background with echo quilting.

Finishing

All seam allowances are 1/4" (5mm).

Block, square and finish the quilt following the instructions on pages 100 - 105.

Embroidery

Bullion 'critters'

Varying the positions and number of insects, embroider the ladybirds and bees in each corner of the centre design after the quilt is pieced and quilted. Stitch insect charms in place among the embroidered bees and ladybirds, sliding the needle between the layers. Stitch rows of beads in place for the trails between the insects in a similar manner.

BULLION BEE

Use two strands of cotton for the embroidery.
See pages 106 - 111 for the individual embroidery stitches. We used contrasting thread for the wings for photographic purposes.

Using yellow, secure the thread and bring it to the front at the position for the head of the bee. Work a bullion knot with twelve wraps.

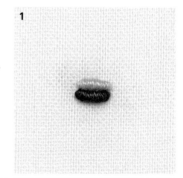

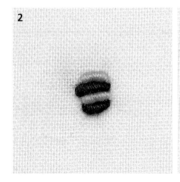
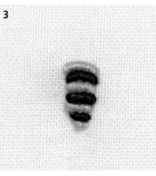
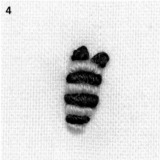
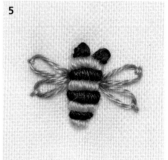

1. Change to black and work a second bullion knot the same size next to the first.

2. Alternating the colours, work two more bullion knots, each with 10 wraps.

3. Alternating the colours, work the remaining bullion knots with 7, then 5 and the last with 3 wraps.

4. Using black, stitch the eyes in French knots, wrapping the thread around the needle three times.

5. Using white, work each wing in detached chain, keeping the stitches relaxed.

BULLION LADYBIRD

Use one strand of cotton for the legs and antennae.
Use two strands for the bullion knots and French knots.
See pages 106 - 111 for the individual embroidery stitches.

Using black, secure the thread and bring it to the front at the position for the ladybird. Work a bullion knot with 16 wraps along the centre of the body.

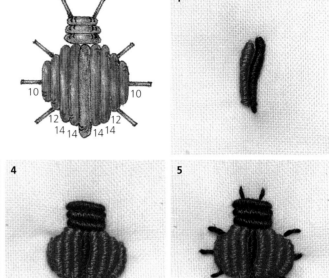

1. Using red, work a bullion knot with 14 wraps just next to the first, from the front end of the body.

2. Work a second red bullion knot next to the first in the same manner, followed by a 12 wrap bullion knot and a 10 wrap bullion knot.

3. Repeat on the other side of the black bullion knot to complete the body.

4. For the head, work three parallel bullion knots, each with 8 wraps across the front of the body, using black.

5. Stitch the legs and antennae in straight stitch.

"Art is man's expression
of his joy in labour."
William Morris

The sampler quilt measures 31^1/$_2$" x 14^1/$_2$" wide (82cm x 37cm).

Miniature Sampler

Several embroideries from the collection of the Art Gallery of South Australia inspired this wall hanging with each block drawing on different design elements. The appliqué is highlighted with gold metallic thread and the blocks bordered using a richly coloured cotton fabric with metallic gold print. The small appliqué blocks would look equally lovely made into cushions or as repeated blocks on a quilt top.

Requirements

Quilt fabrics 44" (112cm) wide

20" (50cm) cream cotton with metallic gold print (blocks, binding)

40" (1m) dark floral feature cotton with metallic gold print (sashing, borders, backing, hanging sleeve)

Appliqué fabric

Fat eighths cotton prints in shades of
Antique gold
Black with red
Cornflower blue
Lavender
Purple
Three shades of green

Supplies

20" x 35 1/2" wide (50cm x 90cm) fusible appliqué paper

18" x 40" wide (45cm x 100cm) piece of cotton batting

No. 9 crewel needle

No. 10 sharps needle

Tracing paper

Fine black pen

Sharp HB pencil

Threads

Stranded cotton
Colours to complement appliqué fabrics

Machine sewing threads
Black or dark grey cotton (bobbin thread for quilting)

Beige (piecing)
Gold and bright gold machine metallic (hand embroidery, quilting)
Monofilament (quilting)

Cutting out

Launder all fabrics before cutting out to prevent shrinkage after the quilt is assembled.

Cream cotton with metallic gold print

Blocks
Cut three, each 8 1/2" (21cm) square

Binding
Cut three, each 2 1/2" (6.5cm) across the fabric width

Dark feature cotton print

Sashing
Cut two, each 1 1/2" x 8 1/2" wide (3.5cm x 21.5cm)

Border
Cut two, each 3 1/2" x 27" wide (9cm x 69cm)

Cut two, each 3 1/2" x 15" wide (9cm x 38cm)

Hanging sleeve
Cut one 7" x 15 1/2" wide (18cm x 39cm)

Backing
Cut one 18" x 40" wide (45cm x 100cm)

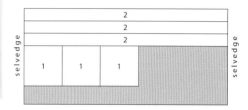

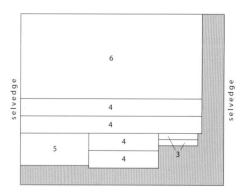

Cutting layouts

Cream cotton with metallic gold print
1. Blocks
2. Binding

Dark feature cotton print
3. Sashing
4. Border
5. Hanging sleeve
6. Backing

Preparation for appliqué

See pattern sheet 1, side 1 for the appliqué designs. Refer to the general instructions on pages 81 and 82.

Trace the appliqué pieces onto separate pieces of appliqué paper.

Referring to the quilt assembly diagram, fuse the pieces to the wrong side of the appropriate fabrics and cut out along the marked lines. Number and group the pieces and set aside.

Preparing the quilt blocks and borders

Fold each block into quarters and finger press the foldlines to mark the centre. Use this as a guide when positioning the appliqué pieces.

Alternatively, transfer the design outlines onto the blocks following the instructions on page 80.

Appliqué

Refer to pages 82 - 85 for general and step-by-step instructions.

Position the appliqué motifs as shown in the diagram, overlapping the shapes as indicated by the dotted lines on the pattern sheet. Fuse the pieces in place as you work.

Using two strands of matching stranded cotton in the crewel needle or one strand of machine metallic in the sharps, work blanket stitch around all appliqué pieces.

COLOUR KEY

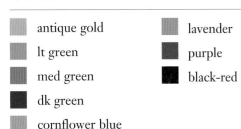

antique gold

lt green

med green

dk green

cornflower blue

lavender

purple

black-red

Embroidery

Using a single strand of metallic thread in the sharps needle, work long straight stitches across the dark flower petals. Work each stitch from the inside edge of the blanket stitch outline towards the centre or base of each flower. Embroider a blanket stitch pinwheel over the centre of the centre flower on the first block.

Piecing and quilting

All piecing is worked using a ¹/4" (5mm) seam allowance.

Piecing the sashing and borders

Referring to the quilt assembly diagram, attach the sashing strips between the blocks following the instructions on page 87. Beginning with the sides, stitch the borders in place following the instructions on page 87.

Layering

Layer the backing, batting and quilt top. Baste them together following the instructions on page 89.

Quilting

All quilting is worked using matching machine quilting thread on the bobbin.

Using monofilament on top, stitch in the ditch around each block and across the ends of the sashing strips.

Free motion quilt around the outline of each appliqué shape following the instructions on page 98.

Change to metallic gold on the top and cross hatch the entire quilt top in a ³/4" (2cm) grid.

Construction

All seam allowances are ¹/4" (5mm).

Blocking and squaring

Square the quilt following the instructions on pages 100 and 101.

Hanging sleeve

Prepare and stitch the hanging sleeve in place at the upper edge, following the instructions on page 102.

Binding

Attach the binding following the instructions on pages 103 - 105.

How to appliqué and quilt

Quilts are made for many reasons including utilitarian, bereavement, friendship and art. There are many rules that are consistent across all areas of quilting. These general instructions focus on the techniques used for the projects in this book and will assist both beginners and experienced quilters with all the information you need to make the quilts and other projects. You can choose to make your quilt entirely by hand or machine, or a combination of both. I recommend that you read the instructions for each project carefully before you begin.

Morris believed that work should be enjoyable and that life, art and occupation should be one. If you look carefully you will find many of my designs are not truly perfect. Have a close look at the Kelmscott quilt where some stems in the repeat blocks fall outwards and some are in a different position. Nature is not perfect and sometimes I think we get too finicky about perfection – remember this is supposed to be an enjoyable process.

Basic Equipment

Appliqué and quilting require only a few basic tools to get started. Always buy the best equipment you can afford. The phrase *'You get what you pay for'* rings true, especially with fabrics and notions. The three things I cannot live without are a sewing machine that has an automatic lift feature of the presser foot (no knee lever or hands required), the needle staying in the down position when the machine stops and an open-toe embroidery or appliqué foot that gives an uninterrupted view of the stitching.

The following information reflects my preferences so that I achieve a good outcome.

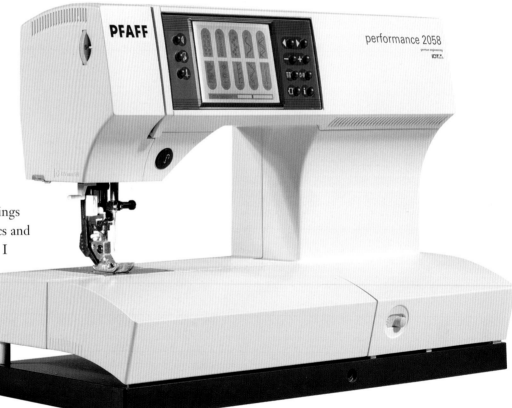

Sewing machine

For machine appliqué you will need a sewing machine with a neat close zigzag, a blanket stitch or other decorative appliqué stitch.
I prefer to use a machine blanket stitch because I find it easier to achieve a neat finish and the stitching is less dense than satin stitch and gives a delicate texture to this, sometimes intricate, appliqué. The less dense stitching also eliminates the need for stabilising the back of the work.

Tension

Adjusting the tension on the upper and lower threads allows you to create even stitches when stitching with different weights of thread such as embroidery rayon and quilting cotton. Always check your tensions whenever you change threads, as different weights need different adjustments. If the bobbin thread is showing on the top of your appliqué the tensions may need adjusting.

Bobbin tension. Check the tension by lifting out your bobbin shuttle. Hold the thread above the shuttle and gently tug it. If the thread shuttle falls away quickly it means the tension is too loose. To tighten, turn the screw very slightly to the right to tighten, 'righty tighty'. If the shuttle doesn't shift at all it is too tight so you need to turn the screw slightly to the left to loosen, 'lefty loosey'.

Top tension. This can be adjusted following your machine manual instructions. If the bobbin tension is adjusted correctly and your bobbin thread is showing on the top then you need to turn your top tension down in numbers. So if 4 is normal you may have to turn tension down to 3 or even 2.

Stitch width and length

The width and length of stitches can be altered to suit your choice of zigzag or blanket stitches. I set my blanket stitch settings to 1.5 width and 1.5 length

Speed adjustment

Having a speed adjustment option on your machine is helpful especially if you are new to this technique. You will achieve a satisfying result particularly around curves if you go slowly, even one stitch at a time on sharper bends.

Feed dogs

When engaged, the feed dogs under the plate move the fabric under the presser foot allowing for smooth tension when stitching straight or smooth lines. For free motion quilting the feed dogs should be lowered to allow the fabric to be moved freely over the plate.

Presser feet

All purpose sewing foot. As the name suggests this foot is used for all general sewing, such as piecing and constructing the quilt.

Darning foot. This foot is used with the feed dogs lowered for free motion quilting.

Open-toe embroidery foot. The open front of this presser foot allows the work beneath to be clearly visible, making it ideal for machine appliqué.

Walking foot. The movement of the walking foot feeds the upper layer of fabric under the foot in the same manner as the feed dogs below. It is used for straight and slightly curved stitching when quilting the layered fabrics.

1/4" foot. All seams must be 1/4" (5mm) wide for accuracy when piecing. This is easily achieved with a 1/4" foot by lining up the edge of your fabric with the edge of the presser foot.

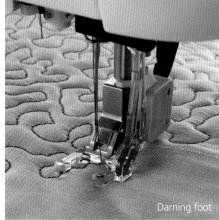

Darning foot

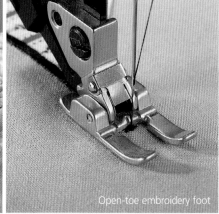

Open-toe embroidery foot

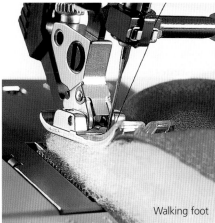

Walking foot

1/4" foot

Rotary cutter, ruler and mat

The *rotary cutter* has a very sharp circular blade allowing for very accurate and straight cutting.
A self healing *cutting mat* is essential when cutting strips and blocks using the rotary cutter.

A *clear ruler* with markings in inches as well as angled cutting lines is an essential tool for cutting strips and blocks accurately.

Bias maker

A bias maker is a valuable tool for making long strips of narrow bias binding, such 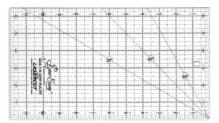 as the binding used for the scrolling pattern on Morris Magic on page 60. They are available in several widths. Cut the bias strips twice the width of the finished bias binding.

Scissors

A pair of small sharp pointed scissors is invaluable for cutting out the appliqué designs. Craft scissors are needed to cut the fusible appliqué paper.

Markers

A *lead pencil* or mechanical pencil is used for tracing the shapes onto the fusible appliqué paper.

A *fine permanent pen* is best for tracing designs onto tracing paper. *Chalk markers* are used to mark the design onto the quilt fabric.

> **!** Avoid using water-soluble markers to mark your appliqué designs. The heat from the iron when fusing the pieces, may cause the marked lines to become permanent.

Needles

Betweens, also knows as quilting needles, are short needles with a small round eye. Used for quilting by hand with sizes 8 - 12 the most commonly used.

Crewel needles, are medium length needles with a large elongated eye used for hand embroidery. Sizes 9 or 10 are best when stitching with one or two strands of thread.

Milliner's or straw needles are long slender needles with a small eye, making them ideal for knot embroidery and beading.

Fasteners

Pins are needed for piecing and constructing the quilts. Always use glass headed pins as they won't melt if passed under the iron.

Safety pins, 1" - 1 3/8" (25mm - 35mm) long, are excellent for pin basting. They allow you to hold the layers of your quilt firmly together without placing your hand beneath the quilt.

Clips

Bulldog clips are helpful for holding backing fabric out flat when you are layering and basting your quilt together.

Other tools

A *thimble* is an essential tool if you choose to work the quilting by hand. It is worn on your middle finger and is used when pushing the needle through the layers.

Small plastic bags, such as freezer bags or snap-lock bags are useful when sorting and storing the prepared appliqué pieces.

Threads

Quilting threads for hand or machine in a colour to complement the fabric is needed for the quilting.

Machine embroidery thread in colours to complement the appliqué fabrics for machine appliqué. My preferred machine embroidery thread is 100% rayon and only suitable for the top thread. These threads are very fine and give a delicate look to the appliqué.

Stranded cotton used in colours to complement the appliqué fabrics if you choose to hand appliqué the pieces and for embellishing with embroidered details and highlights.

Machine cotton in a neutral colour, such as beige or grey is used for piecing the quilt top and for the bobbin for machine appliqué.

Monofilament is a clear nylon thread used specifically for quilting. It is available in two shades – clear for light to medium shades of fabric and smoke for darker shades. Purchase a really good quality thread that is soft to touch and therefore less harsh on fabrics. Monofilament should only be used on the top of your machine – never in the bobbin. Use cotton in the bobbin to match the backing fabric.

> ✳ I find monofilament useful for free motion quilting especially in and around appliqué shapes. It also adds depth and dimension to the appliqué and because it is clear, it can be used in places where I do not want the quilting thread to show.

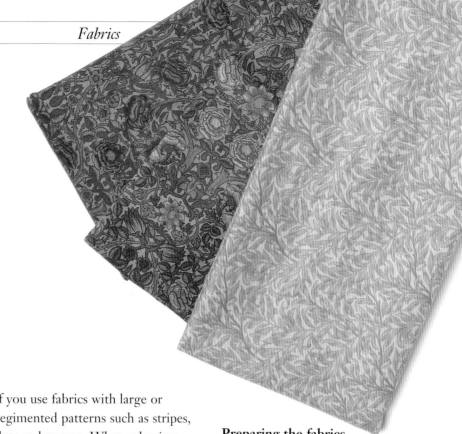

Choosing your fabrics

Patchwork fabrics

Cotton fabrics especially made for patchwork and appliqué are the best and easiest to work with. They are firmly woven, do not fray easily and are easy to cut and press. These fabrics come in an abundance of colours and prints so your choice is almost endless. You may want to keep in mind that many patterns are only available for a limited time and go 'out of print', so if you see something you really love, grab it while you can.

Most patchwork and quilt fabrics are 44" (112cm) wide. Only fabrics sold specifically for backing fabric are at times available in wider widths.

Choosing colours and patterns

Fabrics with small prints in natural colours or tone on tone prints are preferable for my designs. For the most part they are are based on nature and the appliqué paints a picture, which is easily distorted if you use fabrics with large or regimented patterns such as stripes, dots and tartans. When selecting your fabrics think of the textures of leaves, feathers, petals and stems to help you choose.

The instructions for each quilt give you a list with colour descriptions of the fabrics needed. Use this and the colour photographs as a guide when choosing your fabrics.

Preparing the fabrics

Always launder and press the fabrics before you cut out your pieces to prevent the colours from bleeding and the fabrics from shrinking after the quilt is complete.

Trim away the selvedges, if left in a seam allowance they may pull and distort the seams.

Cutting fabrics

The instructions for each quilt give a list of the sizes of all the pieces required for the quilt top, binding and backing. Individual cutting layouts for each fabric illustrate how best to cut the pieces and strips. Cut the strips for borders and binding first to achieve the most efficient use of your fabric.

Fabric pieces can be cut out using either scissors or a rotary cutter. The rotary cutter used in conjunction with a self-healing cutting mat, makes it easier to achieve perfectly straight lines and is the preferred method for cutting strips for borders and binding. The rotary cutter is also quicker to use than scissors, but is not suitable for curved shapes.

Always trim away the selvedges along the sides of the fabric before you cut your strips and blocks.

USING A ROTARY CUTTER

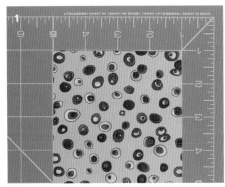 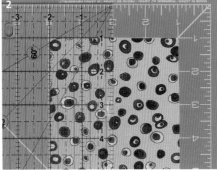 

1. Spread the prepared fabric out on the self-healing mat, ensuring the grain of the fabric is parallel to gridlines on the mat.

2. Position the quilting ruler over the width of fabric you wish to cut, aligning it with the grid lines on the mat.

3. Hold the ruler firmly in place. Starting at the edge closest to you, push the cutter along the edge of the ruler, pressing firmly to ensure you achieve a clean cut.

> * When you need to cut long strips, such as across the full width of the fabric, fold the fabric back and forth in a concertina fashion. Cut across the fold through all layers at the same time.

CUTTING STRIPS

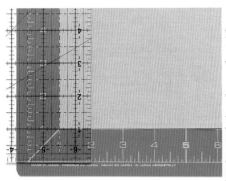

Place the ruler on the fabric so the required strip lies underneath the ruler. The cut edge of the fabric should align with a line on the ruler for its entire length.

CUTTING SQUARES

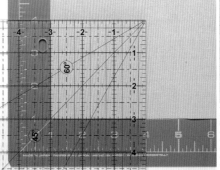

Place a strip of fabric horizontally across the cutting mat. Ensure lines on the ruler line up with both the lower and side cut edges of the fabric.

HALF SQUARE TRIANGLES

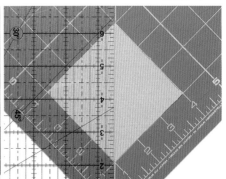

Turn the cutting mat diagonally and line up the square with the gridlines. Ensure the edge of the ruler is aligned with both the upper and lower corners of the square.

QUARTER SQUARE TRIANGLES

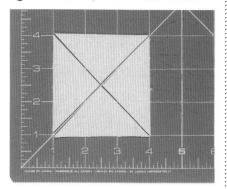

Cut the half triangles as before. Without moving the fabric, turn the mat. Place the ruler across the cut square from corner to corner. Cut to form four quarter square triangles.

CUTTING BIAS BINDING

Binding can be cut on the straight grain or on the bias. If the binding is to be curved, such as the appliqué stems on Morris Magic page 60, cutting the binding on the bias gives the best result.

Preparation

1. The most accurate way to find the true bias is to pull a thread on both the lengthwise and crosswise grain, then fold the fabric to match the pulled thread lines. The diagonal fold created is the true bias.

2. Press the fold and open out the fabric. Measure from the foldline and mark the width of the binding you wish to cut.

3. Leave the ends of the strips tapered or trim them at a right angle to the edge of the strip, depending on personal preference or the technique being used.

Continuous cutting

This method is useful for making very long lengths of bias strips.

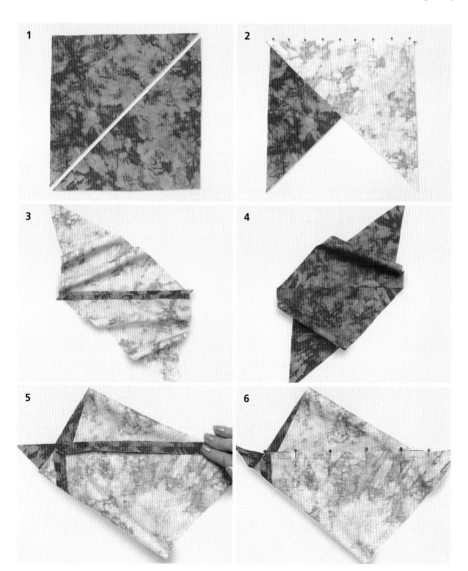

1. Cut a large square of fabric. Fold it diagonally in half and press the fold. Unfold and cut the fabric along the foldline.

2. With right sides together, place the two triangles so the edges meet along one short side of each triangle and the long sides are at right angles. Pin.

3. Stitch using a ¼" (5mm) seam allowance. Press the seam open.

4. Decide on the width of bias strip you require. Rule lines across the fabric parallel to the bias edge, keeping them evenly spaced at the required measurement.

5. With rights sides together, fold the fabric so the diagonal ends meet. Off-set the ends so the first line on one edge is aligned with the edge of the fabric.

6. Pin the ends, ensuring the lines match at the stitchline.

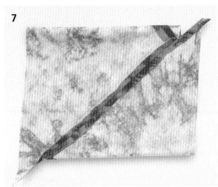

7. Stitch using a ¼" (5mm) seam allowance. Press the seam open.

8. Turn to the right side. Beginning at one off-set end, cut along the marked line through one layer only.

Transferring the design

I prefer to position my designs 'by the eye' but if you prefer you can transfer the design outlines onto the background fabric.

If you choose to transfer the design onto the quilt block or panel, first trace the design onto tracing paper, to achieve the correct orientation and to avoid any design lines from the other side of the pattern sheet to show through.

When transferring large designs, such as Morris Magic on page 60 tape several pieces of tracing paper together to create a piece large enough to accommodate the design. Tape the pieces together, with edges butted, not overlapped.

1. Using a fine permanent pen, trace the design outline and placement marks if required onto tracing paper.

2. Ensuring the orientation of the design is correct, tape the tracing to a window or lightbox.

3. Fold the fabric into quarters and finger press to mark the centre lines. Centre the fabric over the tracing aligning the centre lines with the placement marks if required. Tape or pin in place.

4. Using a sharp chalk pencil, trace the design onto the fabric, tracing just inside the design lines.

> By tracing the design onto the fabric just inside the design lines, the appliqué shapes will hide the lines after placement.

Fusible appliqué

Fusible appliqué paper or paper backed webbing has made appliqué a breeze. The shapes are traced directly onto the paper backing before it is fused to the wrong side of the appliqué fabric. The shape is cut out and the paper removed before the motif is fused to the main fabric and you are ready to stitch the outlines of the shapes.

Follow the manufacturer's instructions when using fusible appliqué paper and always test your paper on a scrap piece of fabric before you begin.

> **!** Always take extra care when ironing your appliqué shapes. Make sure that no fusible appliqué paper extends past the edge of the fabric, so that it accidently ends up being fused to your ironing board. This can easily result in a sticky blackened disaster next time you wish to iron that cream coloured fabric.

TRACING

The shapes you trace onto the appliqué paper when using the fusible appliqué method will appear in the reverse orientation when placed on your background fabric. For instance the bird you traced looking to the left actually ends up looking to the right in your completed quilt. All designs in this book are symmetrical or have been mirrored for your convenience so you can trace them directly from the pattern sheets. Only a few, such as the birds on the Kelmscott quilt on page 40 need to be traced and positioned in a specific orientation.

Use a sharp pencil to trace the shapes onto the paper. Do not cut along the traced lines until after the appliqué paper is fused to the fabric.

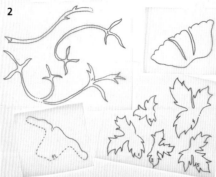

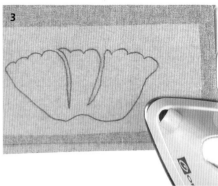

1. Trace the appliqué shapes from the pattern sheet onto the paper side of the appliqué paper. Mark extensions that underlap other pieces with a dotted line. Label all pieces clearly at the edge to assist with colour and placement.

2. Trace all the appliqué shapes that will be cut from the same fabric ¹/₂" (12mm) apart. Work with one pattern and one colour of fabric at a time.

3. Place the appliqué paper, with the paper side facing up, on the wrong side of the fabric. Using a warm dry iron, fuse the paper in place.

4. Cut out the appliqué pieces along the traced line. Do not remove the paper backing until just before positioning the piece on the background fabric.

5. Starting with shapes that underlap other pieces, peel the backing paper away and position the onto the background fabric.

6. Again using a warm dry iron, fuse the pieces in place, using the iron in a lifting and pressing motion rather that sliding it across the surface to avoid shifting the position of the individual shapes.

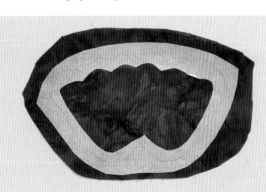

WINDOWING

For larger shapes, cut the paper from the centre of the shape, leaving a ¹/₄" (5mm) rim along the inside edge of the traced line. Also known as windowing, this will make the shape softer in appearance and to touch.

MACHINE APPLIQUÉ

Machine appliqué is most commonly stitched with a close machine zigzag stitch or satin stitch. To imitate the more delicate look of blanket stitch used for hand appliqué, I use a machine blanket stitch to outline the shapes in my designs.

To improve stitch accuracy with an uninterrupted view of the edge of the appliqué shape, work the machine stitching using an open-toe embroidery presser foot on your sewing machine.

Place the machine embroidery thread in the top of the machine with a neutral coloured thread on the bobbin. Test the threads and tension on a piece of scrap fabric to make sure the tension is correct and no bobbin thread is visible on the front of the work.

Anchoring the machine stitches

If your machine has a tie off stitch test this first as I have found it is not always reliable. There are a number of alternative ways you can tie off the stitching at the beginning and end of your work.

1. Pull the threads to the back of your work and tie off by hand.

2. Work a couple of straight stitches before commencing blanket stitch.

3. Turn the width of the blanket stitch to zero before commencing and work a couple of stitches before increasing the width again.

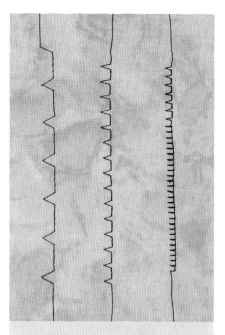

Mock blanket stitch. If your sewing machine does not have a blanket stitch, try adjusting the width and length of the blind hem stitch to achieve a mock blanket stitch.

Machine blanket stitch

Adjust the width and length of the blanket stitch to suit the design and size of shapes you are working on, preferably keeping a consistent stitch size throughout the design. I adjust my default width and length to 1.5 for all my work.

1. Begin at the junction of two appliqué pieces. Stitching the underlying piece first, position the appliqué under the presser foot so that the purl edge of the blanket stitches are along the edge of the appliqué shape.

2. Anchor the stitches at the edge of the appliqué shape using your chosen method. Stitch along the edge of the shape finishing at the edge of any overlapping pieces.

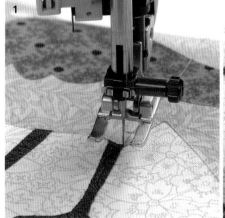

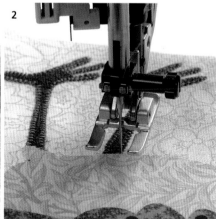

3. Outside corners. Stitch to the corner point, finishing with the needle in the down position on the outside edge of the shape. Raise the presser foot and pivot the fabric to align the adjacent side of the appliqué shape. Lower the presser foot and continue stitching.

4. Inside corners. Stitch into the corner, finishing with the needle in the down position at the edge off the corner point. Raise the presser foot and pivot the fabric to align the adjacent side of the appliqué shape. Lower the presser foot and continue stitching.

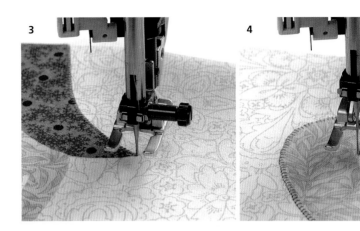

 TAPERED POINTS Stitch in a similar manner to the outside corners. As the shape narrows allow the stitches to cover the full width to avoid fraying the appliqué shape.

HAND APPLIQUÉ

Blanket stitch worked by hand has traditionally been used for *broderie perse* and is ideal for fused appliqué.

1. Secure the thread on the back with a knot. Bring the thread to the front at A, just outside the edge of the appliqué piece.

2. Take the needle to the back at B, through the appliqué piece. Emerge at C, just outside the edge. Keep the thread under the tip of the needle.

3. Continue in this way along the edge of the appliqué piece, keeping the stitches even.

4. Turning a corner. Work three blanket stitches into the same hole to turn a corner or point. Rotate the fabric.

5. Continue stitching in this way to outline the shape.

6. Blanket stitch variation. Slanting the stitch slightly results in a softer finished edge. This variation is used for Bird on page 46.

7. Chain stitch. Work chain stitch following the instructions on page 108, stitching through the very edge of the appliqué shape so the width of the stitches cover the raw edge.

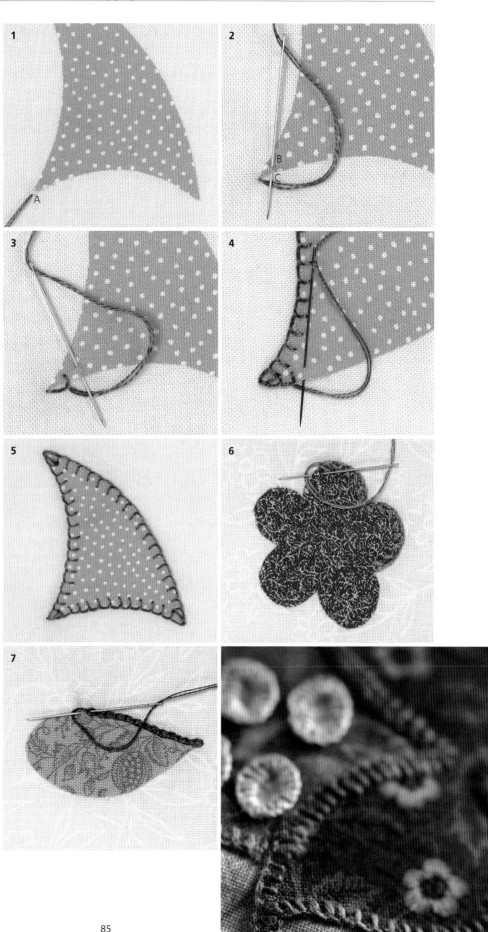

Piecing and quilting

The photographs are designed to provide information about quilting techniques and processes in association with the accompanying text. To add clarity to the pictures, contrasting threads are often used and many of the photographs use samples that are either larger or smaller than what you would normally use when creating your own project. In these instances, follow the instructions in the text even when your eye tells you that the thread colour, stitch length or whatever it may be that is shown in the photo, varies from the written instructions.

Piecing by machine

STRAIGHT SEAM - To achieve even straight seams, align the raw edges of the fabric with a line of sewing machine plate gauge or with the edge of the 1/4" presser foot.

 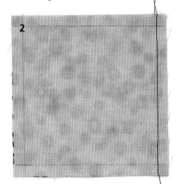 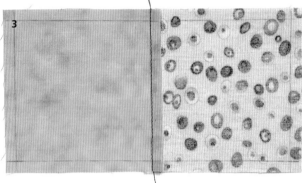

1. Place two pieces right sides together, carefully matching raw edges.
Placing pins at right angles to the stitchline, pin the pieces together.

2. Using a machine straight stitch and leaving a 1/4" (5mm) seam allowance, stitch from edge to edge.

3. Press the seam flat and then to one side.

....

BUTTED SEAM - To achieve a neat finish, it is important that butted seams are accurately aligned.

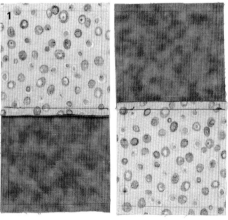 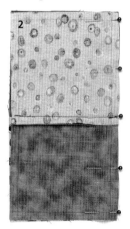 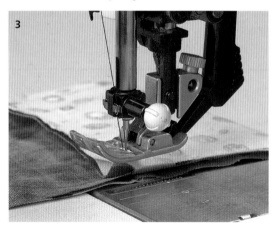

1. Make the required seamed pieces following the steps above. Ensure the seam allowances on the pieces to be joined face in opposite directions.

2. With right sides together and matching raw edges and seams, pin the seamed pieces together.
Ensure the pins are at right angles to the stitchline.

3. Using a machine straight stitch, stitch up to the butted seams. Finish with the needle in the down position.
Lift the presser foot and recheck that the seams are aligned.

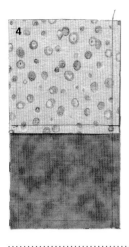
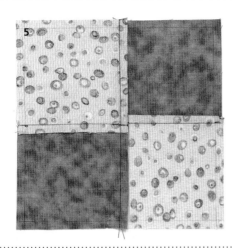
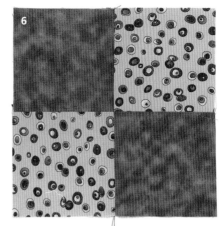

4. Lower the presser foot and continue stitching to the end.

5. Press the seam flat, then to one side.

6. Right side of joined pieces.

SASHING

Narrow strips of fabric are used to create a framework between blocks and borders and is an alternative to setting blocks together.

1. Lay out the blocks and check that they are correctly positioned. Cut the sashing strips to length and place between the blocks.

2. Machine stitch the blocks and sashing strips together.

3. Wrong side. Press the seams flat before pressing the seam allowances towards the sashing strips.

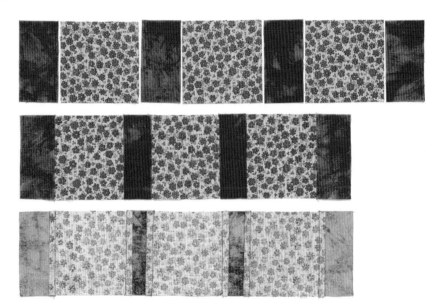

BORDERS

Measuring and piecing borders with butted corners.

The raw edges of an appliqué panel or quilt top may become slightly distorted as you work. It is therefore important to match the length of the borders to the measurement across the centre of the quilt top or panel. Always attach the longer borders before the shorter to assist with squaring the quilt.

1. Measure the length of the quilt top along the centre. Cut two side borders to this measurement.

2. Mark the centre and quarter points along the edge of the quilt top and corresponding border strip with pins.

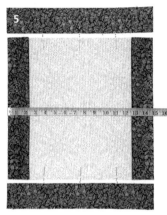

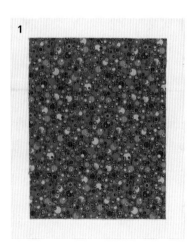

3. With right sides together and matching raw edges and pins, pin and stitch the borders to the quilt top. Ease the edge of the quilt top to fit the border. Press the seams flat.

4. From the right side, place the tip of the iron under the border piece. Move the iron from the quilt top towards the border, unfolding it and pressing the seam allowance towards the border in one movement.

5. Measure the width of the quilt top and borders across the centre. Cut two border strips to fit this measurement.

6. Repeat steps 2 to 4. Continue in this manner for any subsequent borders and sashing strips.

> **!** Always press borders and strips at each step, pressing the seams flat before pressing the border open. The end result will be more accurate and borders will sit better.

Constructing the quilt

PREPARING THE BACKING

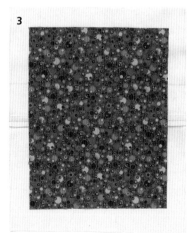

1. Cut away selvedges and press. Cut out the backing to the size of the quilt top plus 4" (10cm) longer and wider.

2. Alternatively, cut lengths of fabric and sew together. Press the seams open.

3. Cut out the backing to the measurements in step 1.

LAYERING QUILTS

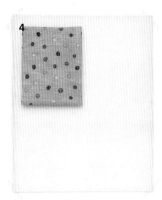
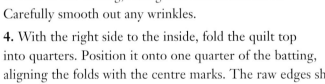

1. Spread the backing out flat, with the wrong side facing up, onto a large flat surface (eg floor or large table). Hold in place with masking tape. Mark the centre of each side.

2. Cut the batting the same size as the backing. Fold into quarters. Position it onto one quarter of the backing. Align the edges and folds of the batting with the backing's edges and centre marks.

3. Unfold the batting, taking care not to stretch it. Carefully smooth out any wrinkles.

4. With the right side to the inside, fold the quilt top into quarters. Position it onto one quarter of the batting, aligning the folds with the centre marks. The raw edges should be an even distance from the edges of the batting.

5. Unfold the quilt top to cover half of the batting. Smooth out with all cut edges an even distance inside the batting.

6. Unfold the remaining half. Carefully smooth it out, taking care not to stretch it or pull it out of shape.

Layering large quilts

To layer large quilts, such as Friends and Kelmscott, place several tables together to create a surface large enough to accomodate the backing with no more than 6" - 8" (15cm - 20cm) hanging over the edges.

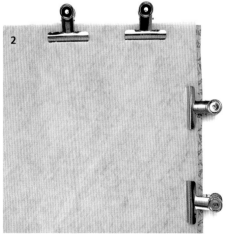

1. Prepare the backing following step 1 above. Ensuring it is smooth and taut (not stretched) hold in place with large clips around the edges.

2. Position the batting over the backing following steps 2 and 3 above. Smooth out from the centre towards each clip. Hold in place with one hand, while re-positioning the clips to hold both layers. Position the quilt top as above.

BASTING WITH SAFETY PINS

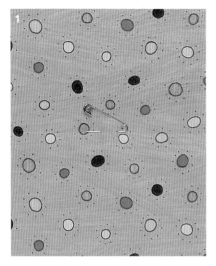

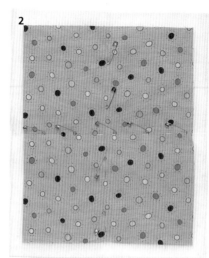

1. Beginning at the centre, take a safety pin through all three layers. Do not close the safety pin.

2. From this centre pin, place pins at regular intervals out to one side and end of the quilt along the centre lines. Place the pins approximately 3" - 4" (8cm - 10cm) apart.

3. Smoothing the quilt top as you go, continue placing pins in one quarter of the quilt. Avoid pinning exactly on the marked quilting lines.

4. Pin the three remaining quarters in the same manner.

5. Close all the pins. Using a teaspoon can make this easier. Slide the bowl under the tip of the pin and twist slightly to lift the tip and catch it.

6. The pins are removed as you quilt.

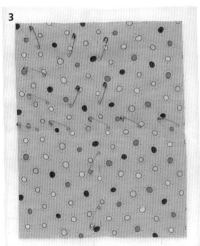

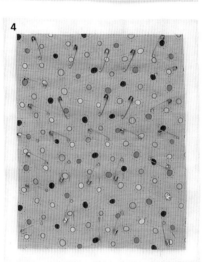

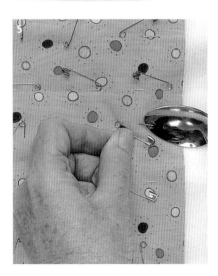

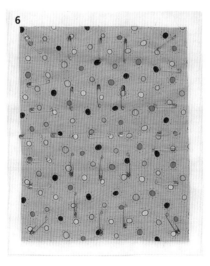

BASTING WITH THREAD

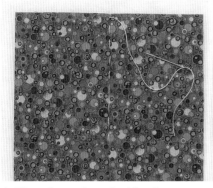

1. Use a long thread with a large knot in the end and a long needle (eg darning needle). Beginning at the centre, work long running stitches to the top of the quilt.

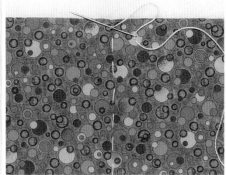

2. End off the thread at the edge of the quilt top with two small back stitches.

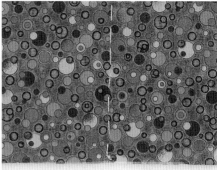

3. Again beginning from the centre, stitch to the lower edge and end off the thread in the same manner.

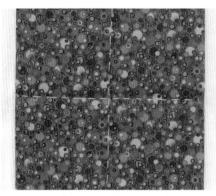

4. Repeat the procedure, stitching from the centre to one side of the quilt and then from the centre to the opposite side.

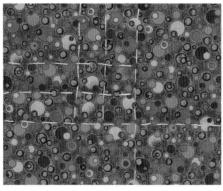

5. Starting near the centre basting each time, begin to fill in one quarter of the quilt with a grid of stitching lines approx 3" - 4" (8 - 10cm) apart.

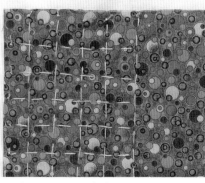

6. Continue until the quarter is completely covered.

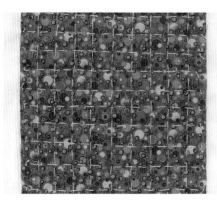

7. Work the remaining quarters in the same manner.

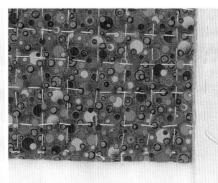

8. Fold the excess batting and lining on one edge onto the right side of the quilt top. Tack in place.

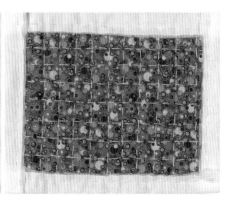

9. Continue around all sides to form a temporary binding. This will help prevent the edges from fraying as you quilt.

Quilting by hand

KNOTTING THE THREAD

This method creates a knot just the right size for quilting.

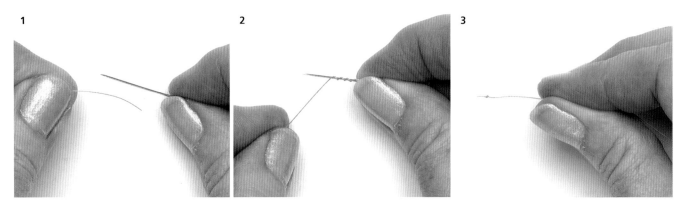

1. Thread the needle. Hold the thread against the tip of the needle approximately 1" (2.5cm) from the end.

2. Wrap the thread around the tip of the needle three times.

3. Hold the wraps firmly and begin to pull the needle through. Pull until a knot forms near the end of the thread.

STARTING THE THREAD

1. Beginning on the right side, insert the needle into the quilt top approximately ⅝" (15mm) away from the starting point.

2. Take the needle into the batting and re-emerge at the starting position. Pull the thread through until the knot lies on the surface of the fabric.

3. Gently tug the thread to sink the knot beneath the surface.

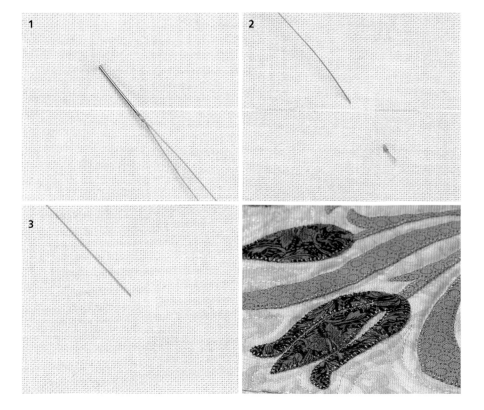

Finishing the thread

1. Pull the thread taut towards you. Hold the needle on the right hand side of the thread so it points towards the fabric.

2. Take the needle over and then under the thread to form a wrap around the needle.

3. Pick up the thread and take it from right to left behind the tip of the needle. The thread around the needle will resemble a figure eight.

4. Place the tip of the needle into the fabric through exactly the same hole from which it last emerged.

5. Take the needle into the batting and re-emerge through the quilt top a short distance away.

6. Pull the thread taut so the knot lies on the surface.

7. Give the thread a gentle tug to sink the knot beneath the surface.

8. Pull the thread firmly to slightly pucker the fabric. Cut the thread close to the fabric.

9. Smooth out the fabric and the tail will disappear beneath the surface.

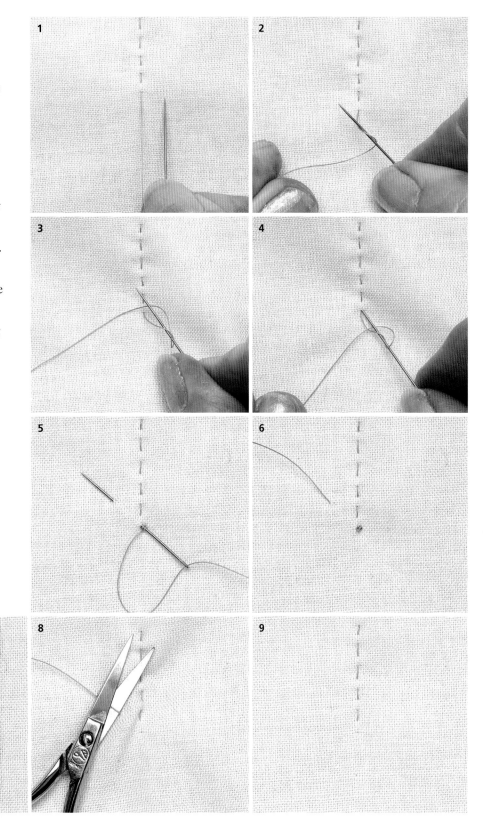

QUILTING WITHOUT A HOOP OR FRAME

1. Place one hand below and one above the quilt and smooth the fabric along the line to be quilted. Pinning through all layers, place several pins across this line.

2. Secure the thread following the instructions on page 92.

3. Firmly hold a section of the quilt in one hand with fingers below and thumb on top. Hold the needle so it lies above your hand rather than below (a bit like holding a pen).

4. Push the needle through all layers until approximately half the needle extends from the back.

5. Hold the needle horizontally. Pull it backwards and run the tip along the lining fabric, with your fingers following, until it is at the spot you want to bring it to the front.

6. Push the tip of the needle upwards with your fingers, applying pressure from the top with your thumb, until the tip is as close as possible to 90° to the fabric.

7. Push the tip of the needle through the quilt.

8. Repeat steps 4 - 7, putting as many stitches on the needle as you can comfortably manage.

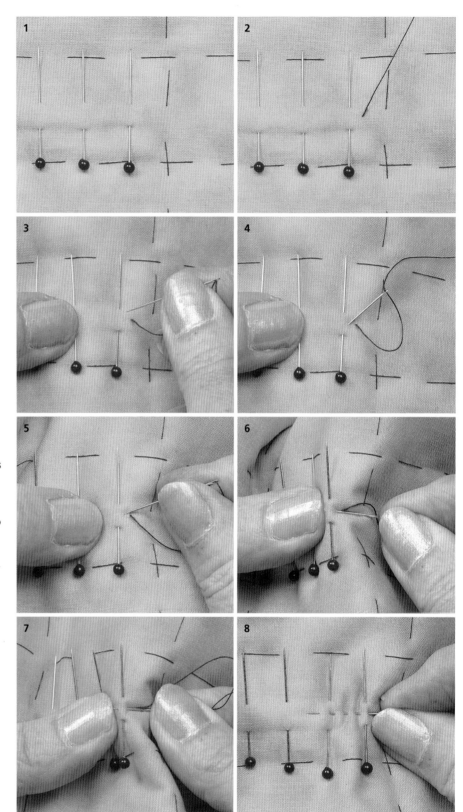

9. Push the needle through with your middle finger.

10. Pull the thread through.

11. Continue repeating steps 4 - 10 for the entire line of quilting.

12. Repeat step 1 before beginning each new line of quilting unless other lines of quilting already stabilize the layers of fabric.

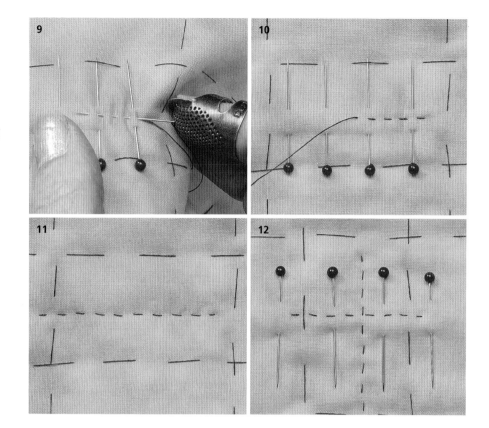

QUILTING WITH A HOOP OR FRAME

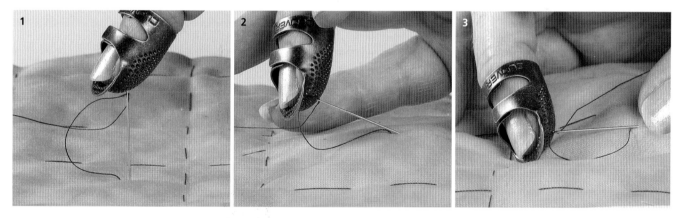

1. With one hand below the quilt, balance the needle at a 90° angle on the top of the quilt. Do not push it through.

2. Gently guiding and rocking the needle with your middle finger only, push it through until you just feel the tip on the underside.

3. Lay the needle all the way back so the tip is pointing upwards. Push upwards with the finger below the quilt while pushing downwards with your thumb at the position immediately in front of the tip of the needle.

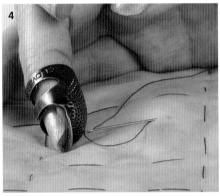
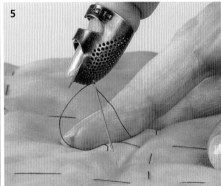
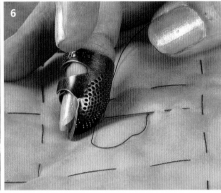

4. Re-apply pressure to the end of the needle with your middle finger to force it back up to the surface. Stop pushing as soon as the tip of the needle is visible.

5. Using the middle finger, gently lift the needle until it is at a 90° angle to the top of the quilt and you can barely feel the tip on the underside.

6. Repeat steps 1 - 5 to place a second stitch on the needle.

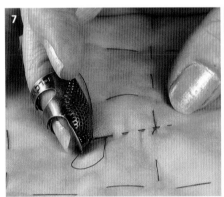
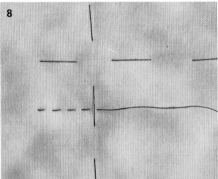
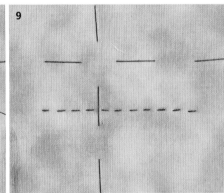

7. Continue repeating steps 1 - 5 until you cannot return the needle to a 90° angle to the top of the quilt.

8. Pull the thread through.

9. Continue repeating steps 1 - 8 for the entire line of quilting.

Quilting by machine

STARTING AND FINISHING

The threads need to be locked in position at the beginning and end of each line of stitching. This prevents them unravelling at a later date and also ensures that your stitching starts and ends exactly where you want it to.

method one

1. Place the quilt under the presser foot and lower the needle into the fabric at the position you wish to start stitching.

2. Set the stitch length to 0. Work several stitches, finishing with the needle in the down position.

3. Adjust the stitch length to the desired length of your quilting stitch and continue stitching.

4. Repeat step 2 to secure the thread at the end of the line.

5. Trim the tails of thread to approximately 1" (2.5cm).

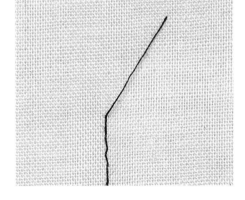

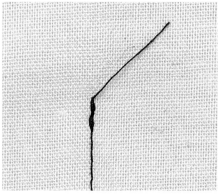 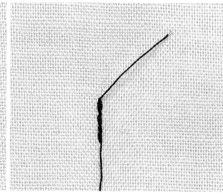

method two	*method three*	*method four*

method two

1. Place the quilt under the presser foot and lower the needle into the fabric at the position you wish to start stitching.

2. Use the securing function built into your sewing machine (if available).

3. Continue stitching.

4. Repeat step 2 to secure the thread at the end of the line.

5. Trim the tails of thread to approximately 1" (2.5cm).

method three

1. Place the quilt under the presser foot and lower the needle into the fabric at the position you wish to start stitching.

2. Set the stitch length to the desired length for your quilting stitch. As you begin to stitch, hold the fabric firmly so it cannot move for the first few stitches.

3. Release the pressure on the fabric and continue stitching.

4. Repeat step 2 to secure the thread at the end of the line.

5. Trim the tails of thread to approximately 1" (2.5cm).

method four

1. Place the quilt under the presser foot and lower the needle into the fabric at the position you wish to start stitching.

2. Set the stitch length to the desired length for your quilting stitch. Work forward for approximately three stitches.

3. Stitch in reverse back to the beginning and then stitch forward.

4. Reverse the procedure to secure the thread at the end of the line.

5. Trim the tails of thread to approximately 1" (2.5cm).

TRIMMING THE TAILS OF TRHREAD

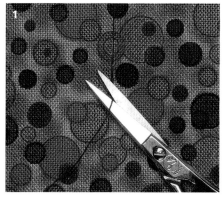 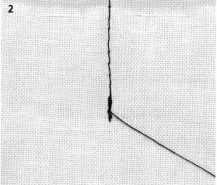 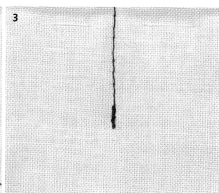

1. Cut the thread on the top of the quilt as close as possible to the fabric.

2. Turn the quilt over. Give the bobbin thread a gentle tug to pull the end of the top thread into the batting.

3. Cut the bobbin thread as close as possible to the fabric.

MACHINE GUIDED QUILTING

This is worked with the feed dogs engaged. Used for straight lines and typically worked before any free-motion quilting.

1. Engage the walking foot on your machine and set the stitch length to 2.5. Secure the threads at the beginning of the stitchline using your chosen method (see pages 96 - 97).

2. As you stitch, hold the fabric on either side, and just in front of the presser foot with both hands to keep it smooth.

3. To work near the centre of the quilt, feed the quilt from left to right under the raised presser foot. Roll up the section of quilt on the right as you feed it through.

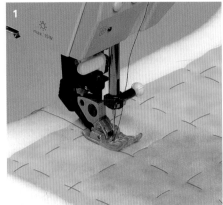
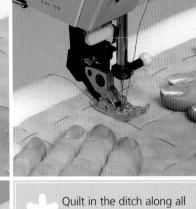
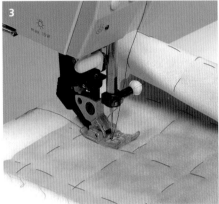

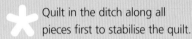
Quilt in the ditch along all pieces first to stabilise the quilt.

FREE MOTION QUILTING

This technique allows you to move the quilt in any direction without turning it. It is ideal for curved lines, echo and stipple quilting.

1. Disengage the feed dog. Attach a darning foot or special quilting foot. Secure the threads using your chosen method (see pages 96 - 97).

2. As you stitch, hold the fabric with both hands held flat and encircling the needle.

3. Maintaining a steady speed, smoothly move the quilt in the desired directions with your hands.

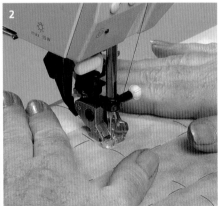
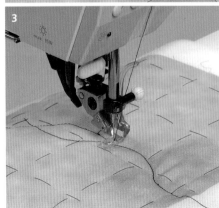

Spend time practicing and experimenting to discover the machine speed and quilt movement that is most comfortable for you.

QUILTING PATTERNS

Plan the route your quilting will take to minimise the number of times you need to end off the thread.

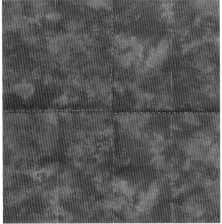

Stitch in the ditch quilting

Stitch in the seamlines around and within the pieced blocks. This is an excellent way to stabilize your quilt. If using this method, it should be completed before continuing with any other quilting.

Cross-hatch quilting

Working backwards and forwards across the fabric, stitch all the lines in one direction, keeping them evenly spaced. When these are complete, stitch all lines at 90° to the first set of lines.

Stipple quilting

This free-motion quilt pattern is worked as a continuous curved line resembling the edges of puzzle pieces. Practise on a scrap piece to achieve smooth, rounded and even shapes.

ECHO QUILTING

This form of quilting emphasises an appliquéd shape and adds movement to the quilt surface. Both machine and hand quilting can utilize this technique.

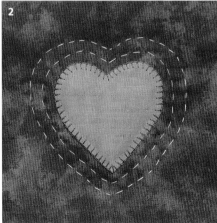

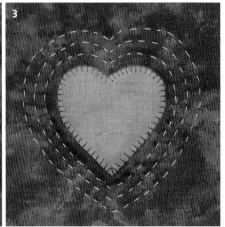

1. Hand quilt around the edge of the appliquéd shape, finishing where you began stitching.

2. Work a second row of quilting, keeping the stitching an equal distance from the shape on all sides. Again, finish where you began.

3. Work a third row in the same manner, keeping it an equal distance from the second line of stitching at all times.

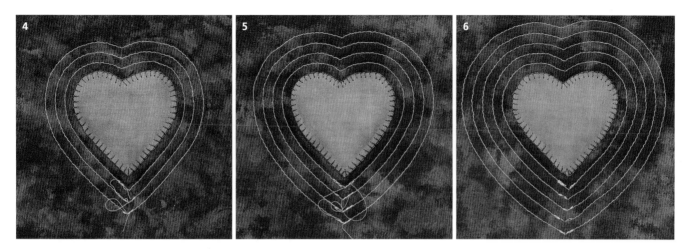

4. If **machine quilting,** lock the thread at the beginning and end off each row but do not cut. Move to the next row, carrying the thread each time.

5. Continue working rows in the same manner, ensuring they are evenly spaced.

6. Trim away the carried threads on both the front and back of the machine quilted quilt.

Finishing

BLOCKING

1. Fold the excess batting and backing over the quilt top and hand baste in place.

2. Hand or machine wash the quilt. Lay the damp quilt on a carpeted floor covered with sheets (or similar flat surface). Remove the basting and smooth out the quilt.

3. Using a metal tape measure, measure the length of the quilt through the centre and along each side. Stretch or ease the sides to match the centre measurement.

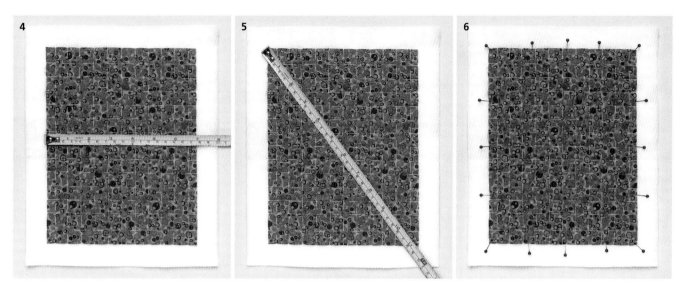

4. Repeat step 3 across the width of the quilt.

5. Measure diagonally across the quilt from corner to corner.
Tug on the corners until the measurement is identical across both diagonals.

6. Smooth the corners so they look square. Leave the quilt to dry.
If required, pin the edge of the quilt to the floor to ensure it remains in place.

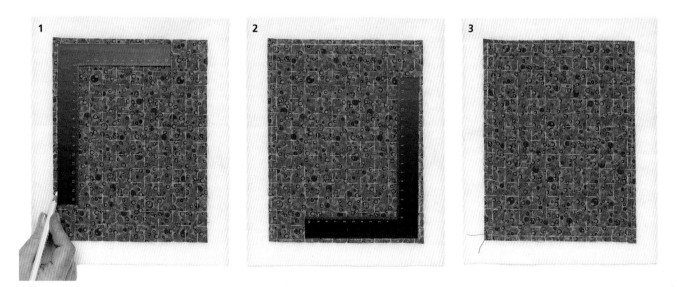

Squaring

1. Using a large square ruler and using the outermost border seam as an additional guide, line up two adjacent sides of the quilt. Rule lines to mark the straight edges of the quilt.

2. Change to a long straight ruler and continue marking in the same manner along the sides. Continue in the same manner around the entire quilt top.

3. Engage the walking foot and stitch a row of machine basting along the marked line. Ensure the needle is down each time you pivot. The quilt is now ready for binding.

HANGING SLEEVE

If your quilt is to be displayed vertically, add a hanging sleeve before attaching the binding.

1. Cut a strip of fabric on the straight grain 9" (22.5cm) wide and 1" (2.5cm) shorter than the width of the quilt.

2. If required, to obtain the desired length, join pieces together and press the seams open. Stitch the edges of the seam allowances down.

3. With wrong sides together, fold under a double hem at each end and stitch in place. Press.

4. With wrong sides together, fold the strip in half along the length.

5. On the wrong side of the quilt, position the raw edges of the strip along the basting at the top of the quilt. Pin in place

6. Stitching through all layers, stitch the sleeve to the quilt just inside the seam allowance.

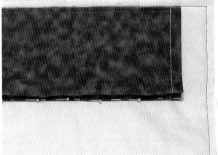

7. At the lower folded edge of the sleeve, make a small pleat. Press.

8. Pin the lower edge of the pleat to the quilt.

9. Hand stitch the lower edge of the ends and the pleat to the lining, ensuring the stitches do not go through to the front of the quilt.

JOINING BINDING STRIPS

Binding strips can be cut on the bias or on the straight grain. To join binding strips cut on the straight grain, stitch at a right angle across the ends.

If the binding is to be curved, bias cut strips are a must. Follow the instructions on page 79.

1. With right sides together, place the ends of two strips at right angles. Allow the ends of the strips to extend beyond each other by approx 1/4" (5mm).

2. Rule a diagonal line across the upper strip from corner to corner. Pin the strips together.

3. Stitch along the marked line.

4. Leaving a 1/4" (5mm) seam allowance, trim away the excess fabric.

5. Press the seam open.

6. Cut off the small triangles of seam allowance that extend beyond the sides of the strip.

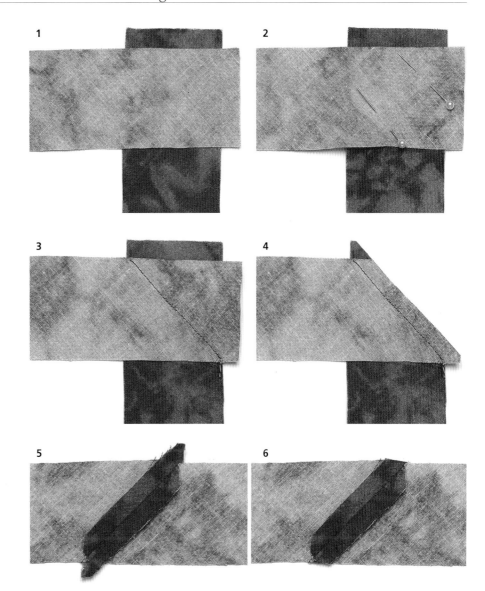

ATTACHING BINDING BY MACHINE - Cut binding strips four times the desired finished width plus 1" (2.5cm).

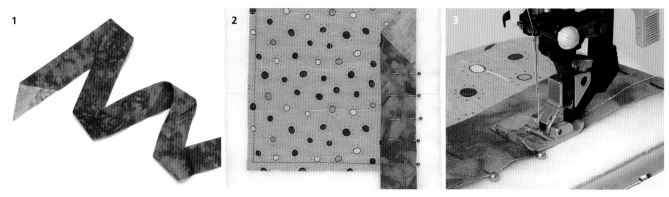

1. Join strips to make one continuous length. With wrong sides together, fold strip in half along length. Press.

2. Beginning near the middle on one side, pin binding to the first corner of the quilt.
Keep the raw edges of the binding and quilt top aligned.

3. Leaving the first 6" (15cm) of pinned binding unstitched, begin stitching towards the corner using
a ¹/₄" (6mm) seam allowance.

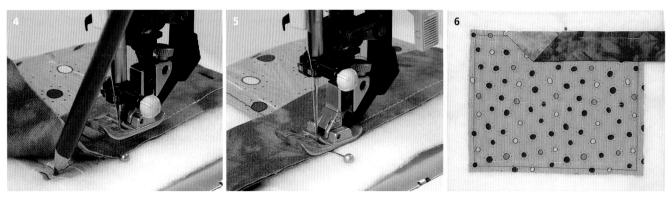

4. When 2" (5cm) from the corner, stop with the needle down. Raise presser foot, turn back binding edge
and mark quilt top ¹/₄" (6mm) in from its edges.

5. Place a pin at the marked spot. Continue stitching until reaching the pin. End off the thread.

6. Remove quilt from the machine and turn it so the stitching is at the top.

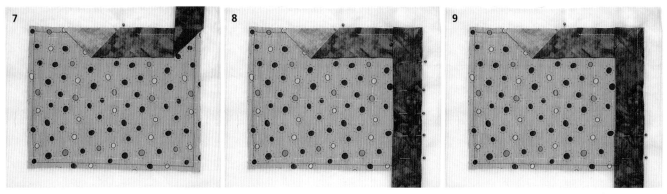

7. Fold the binding strip up at a 45° angle. Press.

8. Fold strip down along adjacent side of quilt top, aligning raw edges as before. Hold fold in place
with a pin. Pin strip to quilt as before.

9. Beginning exactly at the fold, stitch until approximately 2" (5cm) from the next corner.

ATTACHING BINDING BY MACHINE / CONTINUED

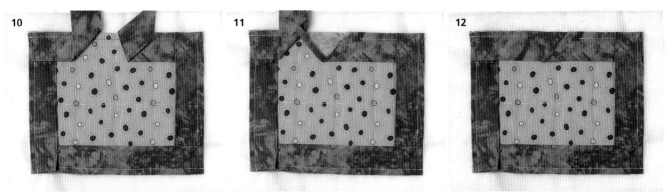

10. Continue around the quilt, forming the corners and stitching until approximately 8" (20cm) from where you first started stitching.

11. Turn under a 1/4" (6mm) seam allowance at the beginning of the binding strip and press.

12. Overlay the end of the strip. Leaving a 3/4" (2cm) overlap, trim away any excess binding.

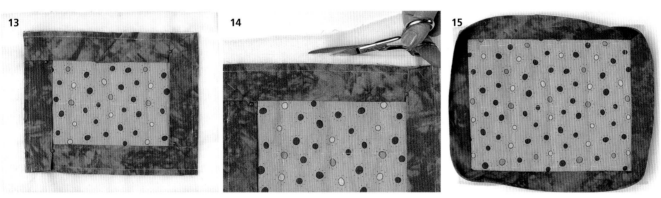

13. Pin and stitch the remaining section of binding in place.

14. Measure out the finished width of the binding from the seamline. Trim away the excess batting and backing fabric beyond this measurement.

15. Press the binding away from the quilt top.

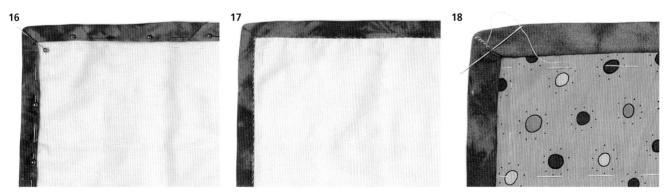

16. Fold binding to the back and press again. Pin the binding in place. Pin the mitres on the back of the quilt.

17. Using thread to match the binding, hand stitch the binding to the backing. Do not take the stitches through to the front of the quilt.

18. Hand stitch the mitres in place.

Embroidery stitches

BACK STITCH

1. Secure the thread on the back of the fabric and bring it to the front at A, a short distance from the right hand end.

2. Take the needle to the back at the right hand end (B). Re-emerge at C. The distance from A to B is the same as the distance from A to C.

3. Pull the thread through to complete the first stitch.

4. Take the needle to the back at A, using exactly the same hole in the fabric as before. Re-emerge at D, on the other side of C.

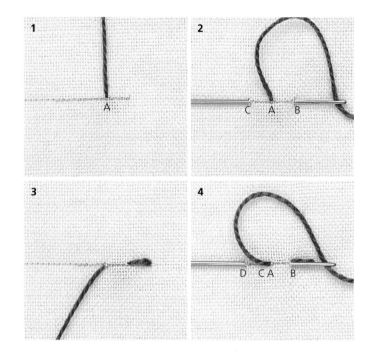

BEADING

1. Secure the thread on the back of the fabric and bring it to the front. Thread a bead onto the needle.

2. Attach the bead and take the needle through the bead again.

3. Pull the thread through. Thread a second bead onto the needle. Take the needle to the back of the fabric at the end of the bead.

4. Pull the thread through. Re-emerge between the two beads.

5. Take the needle through the second bead again.

6. Pull the thread through. Thread a third bead onto the needle.

7. Secure the bead to the fabric in the same manner as before.

8. Continue attaching the required number of beads in the same manner. After attaching the last bead, take the thread to the back of the fabric and secure.

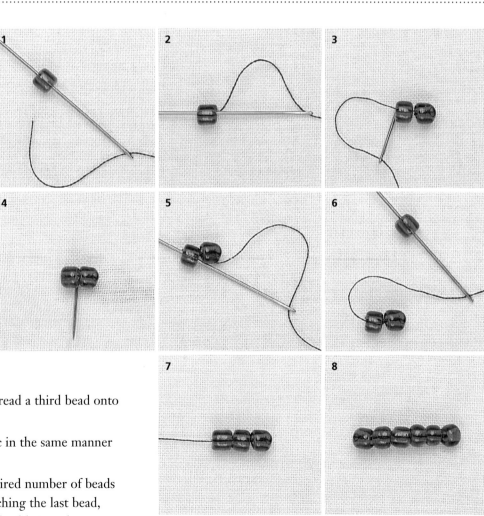

BLANKET STITCH

1. Secure the thread on the back of the fabric and bring it to the front at A.

2. Take the needle to the back at B and re-emerge at C. Ensure the thread is under the tip of the needle.

3. Pull the thread through until it lies snugly against the emerging thread but does not distort the fabric.

4. Take the needle to the back at D and re-emerge at E. Ensure the thread lies under the tip of the needle.

5. Pull the thread through as before.

6. Continue working stitches in the same manner.

7. To finish, take the needle to the back of the fabric just over the last loop.

8. Pull the thread through and end off on the back of the fabric.

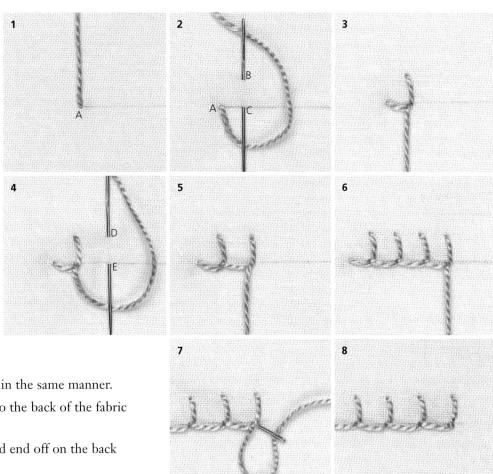

BULLION KNOT

1. Secure the thread on the back of the fabric.
Bring it to the front at A.

2. Take the needle to the back at B. Re-emerge at A, taking care not to split the thread.

3. Rotate the fabric. Raise the tip of the needle away from the fabric. Wrap the thread clockwise around the needle.

4. Keeping the tip of the needle raised, pull the wrap firmly down onto the fabric.

5. Work the required num-ber of wraps around the needle. The number of wraps must cover the distance from A - B plus an extra 1 - 2 wraps. Pack them down evenly as you wrap.

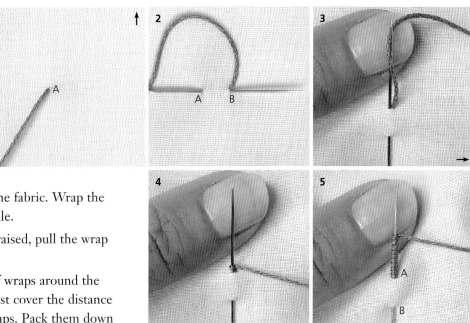

BULLION KNOT / CONTINUED

6. Keeping tension on the wraps with your thumb, begin to ease the needle through the fabric and wraps.

7. Continuing to keep tension on the wraps with your thumb, pull the thread through (thumb not shown).

8. Pull the thread all the way through, tugging it away from you to form a small pleat in the fabric. This helps to ensure a tight even knot.

9. Release the thread. Smooth out the fabric and the knot will lie back towards B.

10. To ensure all the wraps are even, gently stroke and manipulate them with the needle while maintaining tension on the thread.

11. To finish, take the needle to the back at B.

12. Pull the thread through and end off on the back of the fabric.

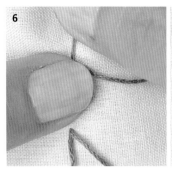
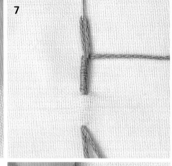
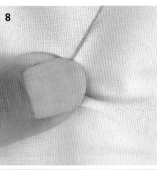
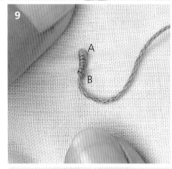
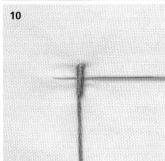
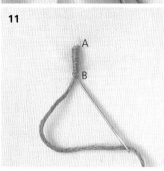
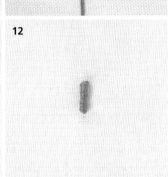

CHAIN STITCH

1. Secure the thread on the back of the fabric and bring it to the front at A.

2. Take the needle from A to B, using the same hole in the fabric at A. Loop the thread under the tip of the needle.

3. Pull the thread through until the loop lies snugly against the emerging thread.

4. Take the needle through the same hole in the fabric at B and re-emerge at C. Loop the thread under the tip of the needle.

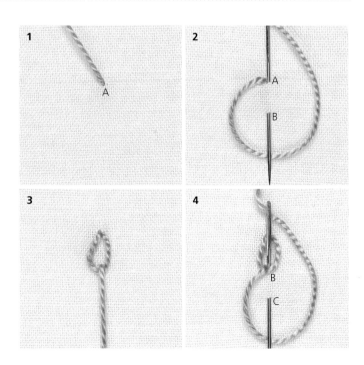

CHAIN STITCH / CONTINUED

5. Pull the thread through as before.

6. Continue working stitches in the same manner.

7. To finish, take the needle to the back just over the last loop.

8. Pull the thread through and end off on the back of the fabric.

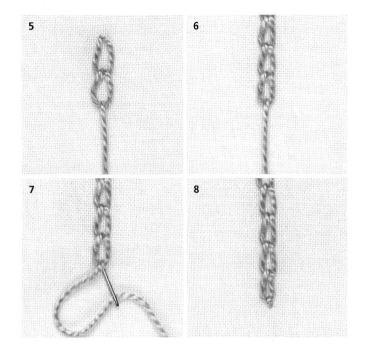

DETACHED CHAIN

1. Secure the thread on the back of the fabric and bring it to the front at A. This is the base of the stitch.

2. Hold the thread to the left.

3. Take the needle to the back at A, through the same hole in the fabric. Re-emerge at B. Loop the thread under the tip of the needle.

4. Pull the thread through. The tighter you pull, the thinner the stitch will become.

5. To finish, take the needle to the back just over the end of the loop.

6. Pull the thread through and end off on the back of the fabric.

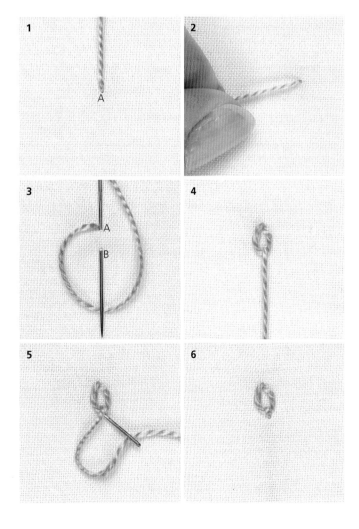

CLOSED FEATHER STITCH

1. Rule lines on fabric. Bring thread to front at A on left line. Pull thread through. Take needle from B to C on right line. Loop thread under the needle tip.

2. Pull the thread through in a downward motion until the loop rests snugly on the emerging thread.

3. Take the needle from A to D, using the same hole in the fabric at A. Ensure the thread is looped under the tip of the needle.

4. Pull the thread through as before. Continue working stitches from side to side in the same manner. Completed closed feather stitch.

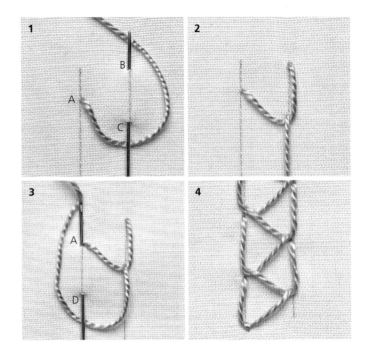

FRENCH KNOT

1. Secure the thread on the back of the fabric and bring it to the front at the position for the knot.

2. Hold the thread firmly approximately 1 1/8" (3cm) from the fabric.

3. Take the thread over the needle, ensuring the needle points away from the fabric.

4. Wrap thread around the needle. Keeping the thread taut, turn the tip of the needle towards the fabric.

5. Take the tip of the needle to the back of the fabric approximately 1 - 2 fabric threads away from where it emerged.

6. Slide the knot down the needle onto the fabric. Pull the thread until the knot is firmly around the needle.

7. Push the needle through the fabric. Hold the knot in place with your thumb and pull the thread through.

8. Pull until the loop of thread completely disappears. End off on the back of the fabric.

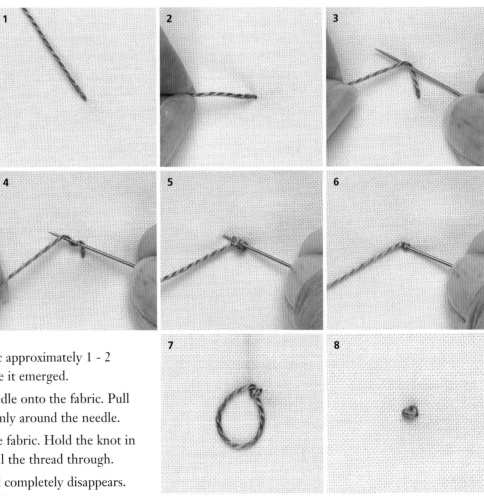

SATIN STITCH

1. Secure the thread on the back of the fabric. Work an outline around the shape using your chosen stitch.

2. Bring the thread to the front at A, just outside the outline and near the centre.

3. Take the needle to the back at B, just over the outline and directly opposite A.

4. Pull the thread through. Re-emerge next to A, angling the needle from under the outline.

5. Pull the thread through. Take the needle to the back of the fabric next to B.

6. Pull the thread through to complete the second stitch.

7. Continue working stitches in the same manner. To finish, take the needle to the back of the fabric for the last stitch.

8. Pull the thread through and end off on the back of the fabric.

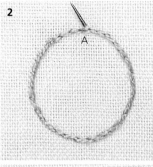
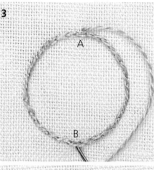
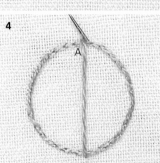
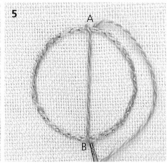
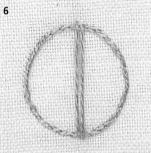
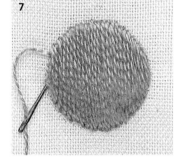
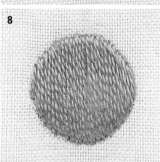

STRAIGHT STITCH

1. Secure the thread on the back of the fabric and bring it to the front at A.

2. Take the needle to the back at B.

3. Pull the thread through. Secure the thread on the back of the fabric.

4. Several straight stitches worked together.

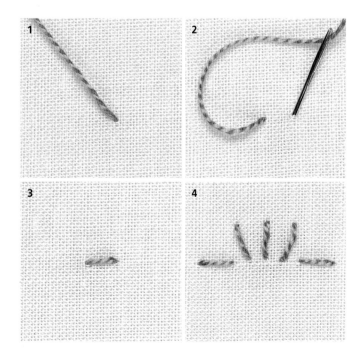

"A Morris design celebrates the natural world". *Michele*

This book would not be possible without the support of so many people.

Firstly, to Anna Scott my editor who shares my passion for all things Morris. Thank you Anna for pushing me along when the going got tough and I was ready to give up and for having the vision to create a book that is a visual feast! My thanks also to the staff at *Country Bumpkin Publications* for their amazing skill and knowledge in making my dream of an appliqué book of William Morris designs come true. To photographer Andrew Dunbar for his expertise – I never knew it could take so many hours to photograph just one quilt!

With deadlines drawing near I wondered how on earth I would ever get the projects completed in time. Three very special friends and quilters; Francie Mewitt, Valerie Pullan and Jill McMahon, whom I had met at my Morris appliqué club, enthusiastically responded to my plea for help with 'no strings attached'. They have all outdone themselves with their workmanship and skill turning my designs into beautiful projects.

Thankyou also to award winning long arm machine quilter Judy Simcock of Cornerstone Creations, who so beautifully machine quilted the Kelmscott quilt.

Thank you to all of you – I am so very grateful.

My thanks also to the many quilters who have contributed to my quilting journey over 20 or more years. To Lee Cleland who so many years ago planted the first seed, to write a Morris book, Gloria Loughman who answered my early questions and Lessa Siegele for her wisdom and knowledge. To special friends who are always there – you know who you are. Your friendship and encouragement is truly cherished.

I also wish to thank Terry and Jennifer Minchinton of Patchwork by Sea, my local patchwork shop, who always know where to search to keep us supplied with wonderful Morris prints. Mark Wilks (Managing Director VSM Aust Pty Ltd) and Pfaff for their continuing support and Barbara Brackman for so generously supplying images from her collection, *A Morris Garden* by Moda. Thank you all for your ongoing encouragement.

My most sincere thanks to the staff at the Art Gallery of South Australia, in particular Christopher Menz (Art Gallery Director) and Antonietta Itropico (Publications Manager). This book would not have been complete without the wonderful images from the Gallery collection. Your support and encouragement is truly appreciated.

To William Morris – I feel blessed that I have had the privilege to reproduce his designs in my own way – long live his genius.

Bird made by Valerie Pullan

Tudor Rose made by Francie Mewitt

Sampler made by Jill McMahon

Kelmscott quilted by Judy Simcock

The Art Gallery of South Australia in Adelaide has one of the world's finest collections of Morris & Company furnishings. In addition to the spectacular tapestry, *The Adoration of the Magi*, the collection includes woven and printed furnishing fabrics, embroideries, carpets, wallpapers, furniture, tiles, designs and stained glass. The collection has developed from furnishings originally purchased directly from Morris & Company for Adelaide houses in the nineteenth and early twentieth centuries. It is wide-ranging in its scope and is recognised internationally. The Gallery's collection of Morris & Company furnishings is featured in the permanent display and has been toured nationally in Australia and internationally.

Morris & Company works from the Gallery's collection are online at www. artgallery.sa.gov.au. The lavishly-illustrated book on this collection, Morris & Co., is available from
The Bookshop,
Art Gallery of South Australia,
North Terrace, Adelaide SA 5000, Australia.
Email: agsa.bookshop@artgallery.sa.gov.au

Morris & Company, London
Britain, 1861 - 1940
Edward Burne-Jones, designer
Britain, 1833 - 1898
J. H. Dearle, designer of floral ground
Britain, 1860 - 1932
The Adoration of the Magi
1900 - 02, designed 1887, London
wool, silk
251.2 x 372.5cm
Morgan Thomas Bequest Fund 1917
Art Gallery of South Australia, Adelaide

Index

Selected Bibliography

- Morris & Company-Pre Raphaelites and the Arts & Crafts Movement
  (Art Gallery of South Australia 1994)
- Morris & Co (Art Gallery of SA 2002)
- Morris & Co – Designs and Patterns (Art Gallery of SA 2003)
- William Morris (Fiona MacCarthy 1994)
- Essential William Morris (Ian Zaczek 1999)
- William Morris - Biography (Fiona MacCarthy 1995)
- Textiles by William Morris and Morris & Co. 1861-1940
  (Oliver Fairclough and Emmeline Leary 1981)
- Textiles of the Arts & Crafts Movement (Linda Parry updated 2005)
- William Morris (John Burdick 1997)
- William Morris Designs and Motifs (Norah Gillow 1995)
- The Beauty of Life – William Morris & the Art of Design
  (Edited by Diane Waggoner 2003)
- William Morris by Himself – Designs and Writings
  (Edited by Gillian Naylor 2000 Edition)

Collections and places to visit

William Morris pieces are held in many places throughout the world, the most significant in Great Britain, US, Australia and Canada. Always contact the museums prior to your visit to make sure exhibits are available.

AUSTRALIA
- Adelaide Art Gallery of South Australia
- Melbourne National Gallery of Victoria

CANADA
- Montreal McCord Museum
- Toronto Royal Ontario Museum

GREAT BRITAIN
- London Victoria & Albert Museum
- London Kelmscott House
- Gloucestershire Kelmscott Manor
- Kent Red House
- Walthamstow William Morris Gallery

UNITED STATES
- California Huntington Library

Websites

www.morrissociety.org/

www.kelmscottmanor.co.uk

www.walthamforest.gov.uk

www.unitednotions.com

www.fabricfreedom.com.uk

www.wmsc.ca/

www.victorianweb.org

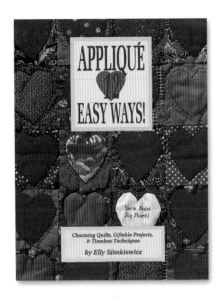

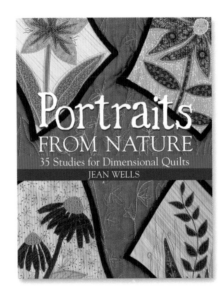

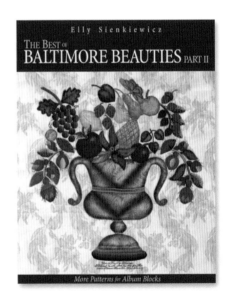

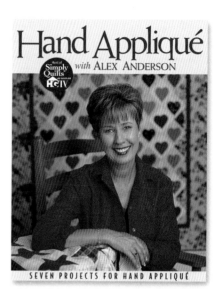

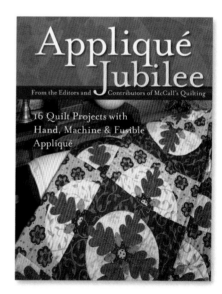

For a list of other fine books from C&T Publishing, ask for a free catalog:
C&T Publishing, Inc.
P.O. Box 1456, Lafayette, CA 94549
Phone: (800) 284-1114 Email: ctinfo@ctpub.com
Website: www.ctpub.com